Astrology's Twelve-Planet Tree of Life

Alice Miller

ISBN-10: 0-86690-662-2
ISBN-13: 978-0-86690-662-3

Cover Design: Jack Cipolla

Published by:
American Federation of Astrologers, Inc.
6535 S. Rural Road
Tempe, AZ 85283

www.astrologers.com

About the Author

Rev. Alice Miller has been a practicing professional astrologer since 1983. Her practice was part time until her second Saturn return and retirement in 1996, and since then it has been her full-time vocation and avocation.

For several years during the 1990s, she taught astrology in Denver, Colorado, creating the texts for her classes. Upon urging from students, she published her first book in 1994, followed by two more in 1995. To date she has completed fourteen manuscripts, initially self-published.

The American Federation of Astrologers began publishing her books in 1999, and continues to bring out beautiful, professional publications of her work. As of this date, six are available from AFA and Amazon.

Rev. Miller also writes for the AFA journal, *Today's Astrologer*.

Readers are invited to visit her website (www.lifeprintastrology.com), where articles, inspirations, and sample readings can be found. E-mail readings and self-published books can also be ordered there.

Books by Rev. Alice Miller

Principles of Astrology: Planets, Signs and Houses

Dynamics of Astrology: Interpreting Aspects

The Soul of Astrology: Inner Dimensions of the Modern Moon

The "Limits" of Astrology: Saturn for Today

Retrograde Planets and Consciousness

Healing the Inner Child: The Astrology of Family Dysfunction

Getting Birth Charts on Target: LMT, Left Dominance, Adoptions

From the Nodes to Fortuna: Journey and Goal

Designs for a New Age: The Grand Cross: Rectangles and Yods

Interceptions : Heralds of a New Age

Intercepted Planets: Possibilities for a New Age

Pagan Astrology for Spirit and Soul

Contents

Introduction

Astrology is the most ancient science in existence. Originally reserved for the wealthy and intellectually elite, its services were exclusively for those in power. To maintain ownership of this valuable tool it was made anathema to the congregations of the dominant religions. Meanwhile, the priesthood kept the secrets of astrology, magic, and other esoteric traditions for their private use. In modern times these studies were further evicted from a place of honor in human history by astrology's offspring. Among those offspring were astronomy and psychology. These proclaimed their superiority in the name of logic, assigning all paranormal abilities to the realm of nonsense.

Today, large portions of the world are recognizing the approach of a new age. Ages are time divisions based entirely on the calculations of astrologers. As always, in periods of great change, the ancient wisdom of astrology rises to the surface of human consciousness. When other thinking structures no longer explain life, astrology forever rises to the occasion, explaining that which is otherwise inexplicable.

Astrology promotes, as its theory of life, the ancient adage: As above, so below. To complete the understanding of the phrase, it is appropriate to examine its other levels: As below, so above; As within, so without. The Creation must reflect the Creator.

If we take Judeo-Christian beliefs literally, humanity is a procreation, living within the creation. Echoing Genesis, Darwin, a scientist, proclaimed that Procreation must carry the genes of the Procreator. This suggests an initial duality in humanity.

Physically, we are a creation and our bodies exhibit the principles of creation. Residing within or behind the physical form is a non-physical being, directly procreated from our Source, containing our spiritual genetic heritage. It is the process by which these principles are established that the language of astrology can first make conscious, then bring to resolution. This is the underlying metaphysics of astrology.

Through centuries of experience, astrologers have established that our solar system provides a symbolic blueprint for life. When viewed from the place of birth, at the time of birth, the map produced can be read as a personal schematic of personality and a master plan the for life of the individual born at that moment. The planets, placed against the backdrop of the signs and seasons, in the context of the hour and minute of birth, are then viewed from the perspective of the birth time date and place. We call this a birth chart or horoscope. It is a personalized version of the basic horoscope of life, which has the equinoxes and solstices at its cardinal points.

We have little logical explanation for why a map of the sky, keyed to a birth, shows so much about our makeup and our lives. Still, science has established connections between the moon and all the fluids of life, especially the tides and female menses. It has also discovered correlations between sun spot activity and radio static. More recently, it has been documented that certain cyclic planetary placements correlate to the cycles of sunspot activity. We may easily theorize from this that there are planetary energies that affect human life in different ways at different times.

More visionary minds may prefer the idea that the Creator, from wisdom or a sense of humor, placed the key to self-awareness in the sky. Perhaps that is why we instinctively look up, searching for God and/or Goddess in the sky.

Thousands of years ago, Jewish Kabbalists established a divine schematic called the Tree of Life. Composed of Sefirot, it was drawn into a specific design to show the relationships of the Divine qualities to be sought within humanity. Legend says that the Divine tree has its roots in the Heavens, while the human tree has its roots in Earth. The two touch at the head or top of the tree.

The design of the Kabbalah, as drawn, resembles a tree very little, and may remind us of the sky constellations, which often require considerable imagination to perceive the named forms. Interestingly enough, there are ten sefirot in this tree. In modern history, astrologers have also used ten planets in horoscopes.[1]

Like the Sefirot, they are used to symbolize qualities of being and human development. Unlike the Sefirot, the growth, awareness, and spiritual development of humanity has been included in horoscopes by using more recently discovered planets to symbolize it.

Until the 1700s, only seven planets were visible to astronomers, so only those seven were used in horoscopes. Then as human consciousness began its rise with the industrial revolution, more planets were discovered, providing new symbols for new qualities of being. Uranus was discovered in 1781, Neptune in 1846, Pluto in 1930, and Chiron in 1977. These bring the list of planets up to eleven. Since there are, and always have been, twelve signs, we assumed that there was one human quality, and a planetary symbol for it, still to be discovered, and that it would be the new ruler for Libra. Finally, in January of 2005, a twelfth planet was discovered and eventually named Eris.

The first three planets in the *modern* category were found in orbits of increasing distance from the sun. Chiron, on the other hand is small, and was discovered among a group of asteroids, suggesting a quality present all the while, but only recently noticed or named. Meanwhile, Eris had been *hiding in the distance*.

---

[1]Astrologers include the Sun and Moon as planets and omit earth because it is the point of observation for the horoscope. T his produces a geocentric, or earth-centered, chart, which is psychologically and spiritually valid. It is not intended to be objectively valid.

Her orbit lies far out beyond that of Pluto, where she seems to be stretching out to reach the stars.

While most planets have circular orbits, only Pluto, Chiron, and Eris have oval ones, causing their aspect-rhythms to vary. This type of orbit allows for widely different levels of personal effects on individuals, and is probably related to individual incarnational history and personal evolution. By viewing the planetary energies in a Kabbalistic fashion, it is possible to get a sense of how human consciousness evolves, both at the individual and species-wide levels.

Theory and Structure

This design groups the planetary principles in three columns and several rows (see table). The center column is the Identity Structure, with the Consciousness Structure on one side and Creativity Structure on the other.

At the top-center of our chart is the Sun. Just below, and on either side, are Mercury and Venus. This is to show that there are two planets between the Earth and the Sun. They symbolize solar radiation. The Sun emits light/Mercury and warmth/Venus. Think of it as electromagnetic with light as the *electo* and warmth as the *magnetic* elements of our electromagnetic system. In this placement, as the rulers of Gemini and Taurus, Mercury becomes generic intelligence and Venus becomes generic attraction/creativity—the ability to create or add value to our own lives by attracting substance of value.

Channel all this through the Moon, into the Ascendant/wheel, and spirit becomes incarnate form. Moving beyond Earth, the remaining planets, expressed through the signs they rule, show how we project energy outward. As we have received from Sun, Mercury, and Venus, through the Moon, so we give through the planets beyond Earth, personally and to Society/Earth under the auspices of Mars, as poured through the next four portals: Chiron—as the human expression of Mercury and Eris—as the human expression of Venus, together with Jupiter and Saturn.

Moving beyond our Social phase, we give impersonally to God/dess and/or the Universe, under the auspices of Uranus, as poured through Neptune and Pluto.

Mercury	Sun	Venus
Divine Light	Life	Divine Warmth/Love
Universal Intelligence	Divine Spirit	Universal Substance
Direct Current	Energy-Radiation	Magnetic Charge
Light as Wave	Electro-Magnetic	Light as Particle
	System	
	(Son/Daughter of	
	God)	

Moon
Soul
Transformer
Channel, Blueprint

Earth
Humankind

Chiron Mercury	Mars	Venus
Human	Human Spirit/Energy	Human Love
Consciousness	Incarnation	Spacial Relationship
Mental Organization	Survival Instinct	Value Judgments
	Son/Daughter of	
Jupiter	Man	**Saturn**
Expansion/Growth		Safe Limits
Principles/Beliefs/		Responsibilities and
Ideals		Rights
Enthusiasm		

Neptune	Uranus	Pluto
Mystical (Sub)-con-	Extended (Galactic	Creative Conscious-
sciousness	and Divine) Out-	ness
Expanded/	reach	Directed Personal
Unbounded	Humanity Radiating/	Reality
Awareness	Reaching Outward	Unlimited Personal
Boundless	(Son/Daughter of the	Power
Knowledge	Universe)	

The Identity Structure: Sun

At the top-center of our chart, we place the symbol for the Sun. It represents the Son of God placement, as the Father figure, especially the progenitor of our spiritual DNA. As a metaphor, think of the double helix as one strand for spiritual heritage and one for physical heritage. The Sun represents the *Heavenly Father*, especially as the divinity that resides in us. It represents your spiritual heritage as Son or Daughter of Divinity.

The Sun represents the divine incarnating Spirit, the underlying motive for incarnation. This determines the kind of energy you will *run on* during the incarnation. It establishes the parameters of the electro/consciousness-magnetic/creativity system.

Your chart, your life, runs on the kind of energy described by the Sun's sign. You may not look like your Sun's sign (few people do), but its energy type will underlie all that you do. If it does not, your first lesson will be to reclaim your Sun. To fine tune your chart, consider this energy type when interpreting your planets, for each of them is powered by Solar energy, as directed through the lunar transformer.

Sun in the Elements and Signs

Sun in Fire

Fire Suns radiate pure Spirit, sometimes ignoring body. They get fired up and take off running, often impulsively. They burn brightly, keeping life moving steadily onward and upward.

Aries: The Aries Sun radiates pure, uncontaminated spirit/energy. Aries represents absolute innocence. It is motivated by survival instincts and/or a pioneering spirit. These people are courageous and indomitable, the catalysts of the zodiac. To them belongs the title Son of Man.

Leo: The Leo Sun radiates pure light. It is motivated by the urge to shine and/or to display inherited qualities, talents, status, etc. These people identify as spirit, acting in/as/through form according to whether they regard their origin as human or divine. To them belongs the title Son of God.

Sagittarius: The Sagittarius Sun expands from its core, like the Sun's corona. It is motivated by the joyous, enthusiastic urge to expand awareness and/or experience. These are the messengers carrying the good news that we are more than we once believed ourselves to be. To them belongs the title apostle or angel.

Sun in Earth

Earth Suns are attractive. They run on magnetism, attracting needed substance for creating reality. Realizing the necessity for a body to facilitate spirit's activities and intentions, they solidify spirit/energy into forms of value and usefulness, as living proof of humanity's manifest destiny.

Taurus: The Taurus Sun carries a strong and steady magnetic charge that naturally condenses into whatever is of value to it. It knows its worth and because it does, it naturally attracts money and other goods. It is the living principle of *like attracts like*.

Virgo: The magnetic field of the Virgo Sun attracts useful opportunities and experience necessary for a healthy body and lifestyle. Natives know what is useful and how to use it for the greater good. Their most important lesson is that they are servants of no human, but rather *servants of the most high.*

Capricorn: The magnetic field of the Capricorn Sun attracts the mature/noble/honorable substance of public image-reputation, authority, respect. These are independent spirits, the adult offspring of deity. They truly have *dominion over the Creation.*

Sun in Air

Air Suns identify as a Consciousness. Their energy is dual, like alternating current. It functions through the physical and nonphysical senses. The physical senses seek consciousness through relationship, defining relationships by the amount of space in them. The nonphysical senses regard air as the vehicle for light, and the pursuit of enlightenment, at one level or another, is a recurring theme.

Gemini: The Gemini Sun is the student and/or communications expert of the zodiac. They are the *witnesses and namers* of Creation. They are the questioners that keep human consciousness expanding.

Libra: The Libra Sun is the reflector and partner of spirit. They do not have a human *other half*, but are the *other half* of the creation. This is truly one *made in the image of the Creator*, and reflecting that creativity onto Earth.

Aquarius: The Aquarius Sun is of the galaxy and of the future. Friend to God and Man, these are linked into universal consciousness. In some way each is a priest/tess, standing between Heaven and Earth, in communication with both.

Sun in Water

Water Suns run on emotional energy. More accurately, they are powered by the human need system. Emotions are the (muscular) action of expressed feelings. Feelings are the mind of the body, communicating physical needs. Activity is impulsed by needs of self and/or others. Energy is fluid. It takes on the shape of its (Saturnian) container, and finds its own level.

Cancer: Cancer runs on the most basic need—the need for visibility, to be born into this world. Cancer holds a very strong growth impulse, not always well-disciplined but virtually unstoppable. Cancer grows for all of its life. Sometimes Cancer power is latent, but it is always present and subject to demand.

Scorpio: Scorpio runs on passion, an adult energy. Scorpio is often expressed as the need for power (not control)—literally the power to create life. Scorpio is also about intensity—the kind of intensity needed to create, to work magic. It is pure *force* and neither good nor evil. Think of steam power, or dynamite—the best or the worst, depending on how it is used.

Pisces: Pisces runs on mastery, and much of their lives happen automatically as a result of what they are, not what they do. They need periods of withdrawal, even as they complete their current evolutionary course. Having mastered the current cycle of incarnation, they are preparing for rebirth in Aries.

***

If the Sun is unconscious, as when it is placed in the twelfth house or in an interception, your life may seem underpowered until you make it conscious. Technically this happens as the Sun progresses from the twelfth to the first, or when the interception is opened by a transit conjunct, opposite, or occasionally square, the Sun's sign.

Suppression usually comes from conditioning. When the Sun is in the twelfth house, we are required, in the name of survival, of getting needs met, and/or of getting approval to forget our true selves. Interceptions hide planets largely because they represent a quality, or the evolutionary level of that quality, which is an unknown in the birth environment. Interceptions often show conditioning that teaches you that there is something wrong with that sign and/or planet, that it is impossible, crazy and/or immoral to be what it is. This always shows that the native is in some ways *older*/more evolved than the people who surround our early years. Consequently, much of their power is hidden until later in life.

Two other placements are especially difficult. When the Sun is in the seventh house, it gets projected onto other people. Someone in your childhood models difficult sides of the sign with enough force to make you reject it. Traditionally, the Sun has represented the human father—for many, the man who gave you your surname. For older natives, the difficulty of this placement came from being conditioned in such a way that we believed that we could not be like our father, or an experience of him that causes us to reject him (internally and/or externally).

This qualification seems not to hold true for Indigos and Crystals, whose charts have much less of the human parents in them. Perhaps this is because they easily accept the fact of their spiritual heritage and of having a Divine Father. We are, after all, both physical and spiritual, with two sets of DNA. Without the divine DNA, there can be no physical DNA, and vice versa. Today, the newer generations of humanity are born with a clearer sense of that. They may understand the need to claim seventh house placements, even while concentrating on a use or an expression of the sign that differs from the (parental) model.

The Sun in the eighth house is conditioned to think of the Self, the father, and/or your Sun's sign as *not good* . . . maybe *not good enough*. This teaches self-condemnation, and can lead to low self-worth. The good side of this is that the eighth is simply *not good for children* . . . like sex.

The eighth is a transformative house: any time you claim your adult status, you can also reclaim the good side of your Sun and its sign. Planets in the eighth are adult assets and once adulthood has been fully claimed, they function as positively as second house planets.

Basic Consciousness: Mercury

The twin expressions of the Solar energy are Mercury and Venus. Mercury is subjective and intellectual, designed for expanding awareness. Venus is objective and tangible, designed for creating reality. Mercury is light as waves. Venus is light as particles.

Mercury heads the Consciousness column, which might be called our internal computer. In that sense, by sign, Mercury describes the type of consciousness that we have. Lying between the Sun and the Earth, it is a function of our spiritual being. If you are alive, you are conscious. It symbolizes our potential to awaken self-awareness through incarnational experience.

Mercury is a dual/twin energy. Physically, it represents both the brain and the senses, and specifically the eyes. Ultimately, it is the perceptual or data-enter function. Think of the phrase, "I see. . . ." Mercury aspects define our senses, especially our vision. Negative ones may show visual dyslexia or other seeing problems.

Another dual quality is the concept of *data in-data out*. Mercury is words (and numbers), the verbal symbols for reality. It is the most significant element in communication, and consequently, a primary factor in relationships of all kinds. It refers to the way we name things, the questions we ask, and our preferred style of learning, and it often indicates what we wish to learn.

Mercury in the Elements and Signs

Mercury in Fire

Fire Mercury can be almost *greedy* for learning, especially self-awareness. These are quick minds full of intellectual fire. These minds are seldom still, even when the body which they inhabit is in repose.

Aries: Aries Mercury is a survivalist first, and some remain fixated there. Most go on to explore the new and untried. They are *thought pioneers* who frequently evolve into *seed beings*.

Leo: Leo Mercury is less adventurous, being vested in heritage, role, and image. Leo seeks to correctly speak the proper lines. They do not so much generate ideas as they shine light upon existing thought. Most can quote other thinkers.

Sagittarius: Sagittarius Mercury will take an idea and run with it. He is forever crossing boundaries of language and belief as he follows principles to distant applications. Confirming Mercurial duality, he can also ferret out the principles behind applications.

Mercury in Earth

Earth Mercury thinks practically. Ideas must hold substance, must be productive. This is a tenacious mind, sometimes resistant to change. At its best, it constructs useful, proven, concepts that endure.

Taurus: Taurus Mercury is value oriented, a creative mind, fixed on practical issues. She will not *waste time* on ideas that have no profit potential. Taurus is the builder and the banker of the zodiac, the maintainer and sustainer of life.

Virgo: Virgo Mercury is service and use oriented. Ideas must serve a useful purpose. They must work. Virgo is the efficiency expert and healer of the zodiac; s/he makes things work right. As Virgo Mercury evolves, she may discover that her most useful tool is intuition.

Capricorn: Capricorn Mercury is serious-minded, oriented to practical wisdom, to ideas that have proven to be practical and valuable. Capricorn Mercury is a good manager, who may combine logical and intuitive processes, assigning tasks according to abilities. He may integrate more intuition to his thought processes than he will admit.

Mercury in Air

Air Mercury shows a mental, often an abstract, approach to life. This is the thinker, the questioner, the student of the zodiac. Their great task is learning the power of names, and the technique called, "Name it and claim it." They ask the questions and propose the theories that lead to greater knowledge.

Gemini: Gemini Mercury is very dual and refers to *data-in, data-out*. A very active mind that sometimes runs out the mouth! Gemini collects information, but may do little with it. They just want the facts! This placement often confers an encyclopedic mind.

Libra: Libra Mercury is about mental balance or imbalance. Their ability to see both sides of an issue is legendary. It frequently interferes with choice-making. The balance intended is between right and left brain, which *married* can form the union known as conscious channeling. When this occurs, the mind may shift levels quite seamlessly to produce a medium.

Aquarius: Aquarius Mercury is about original thinking. Often this means future-oriented, as these genius minds are ahead of their times. From this comes the notion of a fine line between genius and insanity. Sometimes they are called insane because of their ability to draw inspiration and invention from the distant realms of time and space. A few actually create that. It is critical for Aquarius to accept its differences, to realize that its originality is what keeps life evolving.

Mercury in Water

Water Mercury is fluid and *feels its way through* by a thinking-style that can look more like the Moon than Mercury. This Mercury is more tuning device than perceptive tool. Most are empathic and many channel information from invisible sources, rather than perceiving it from visible ones.

Cancer: Cancer Mercury is clearly Moon-dominated. This means that thinking is conditioned by needs. Information seems to flow to natives, as they need it.

Scorpio: Scorpio Mercury is powerful and penetrating, rather like a laser. Scorpio is quite adept at *calling up* information at will. Most can *read people*, see through pretense. They can also be powerful speakers, almost hypnotic. This comes from the ability to concentrate and control mental focus into a tight *beam*.

Pisces: Pisces Mercury knows no limits or bounds. It acquires information by osmosis, soaking up much subliminally. Having mastered the full spectrum of consciousness, the mind is no longer sharply divided. Right and left brain functions may blend, making logical process so fast that it blurs. Pisces *just knows*, and cannot explain how it knows—largely because spoken language is inadequate for doing so.

***

For *students of consciousness*, look to the planets Mercury, Chiron, Jupiter and Neptune, and the signs they rule, along with their relationships/aspects for guidance. This shows something about how you process information. It is important to notice the relationship between houses three, six, nine, and twelve and these planets. This will show how your conditioning does or does not support your ability to expand your awareness. Some lessons can be adapted. Others must be rewritten using various forms of prayer, as affirmations, visualizations, and/or rituals.

Attraction: Venus

The twin expressions of the Solar energy are Mercury and Venus. Mercury is subjective and intellectual, designed for expanding awareness. Venus is objective and tangible, designed for creating reality. Mercury is light as waves. Venus is light as particles.

Venus represents, first and foremost, the principle of magnetics. It is the bond that holds bodies in form. It is the root of the maxim, *Like Attracts Like*. More importantly, like thought attracts like thought and with sufficient concentration of like thoughts, visible, tangible creation occurs. This is why Venus heads the creativity column.

The actual essence of the creative consciousness is a concentration of focus. The more we focus on a thought, desire, hope, wish or dream, the sooner it will become manifest reality. Each thought has a magnetic charge, some with more energy than others. But once you have thought or spoken a desire, hope, wish, or dream, it will attract more charge each time it is repeated. Thus it may acquire sufficient energy for manifestation through a group ritual and/or through repetition by an individual.

This is where the idea of Venus as a planet of love originates. Those things we love, those things we value, are naturally attracted to us. The more we love them, the more we desire them, the more often we hope, wish or dream of them, the quicker they will manifest . . . if we hold no hindering beliefs. The sign in which your Venus is placed suggests those things that are innately conscious values for you and which will most easily be created.

From this comes the connection with self-worth. If we are to attract anything, we must believe that it is good for us and we must feel worthy of having it. We must believe that we are entitled to it.

You must see yourself as good if you wish to attract good things into your life. If you are to achieve wealth, you must believe that wealth is holy and that you are good enough, that you deserve to have it.

A key understanding here is that (using Christian terms) in the beginning all of the creation was named "good and very good" by the Creator. The other is that we are the literal offspring of our Creator, and thus we inherit creativity through our *spiritual DNA*.

We must also agree that it is good for us to have what we wish to draw into our lives. We must claim our spiritual heritage and purpose, believing that we deserve the very best. Out of this comes the difficulty which some have of being afraid to ask for, or attempt to create, things because of what will come with them. If you pray for something (prayer includes affirmation, visualization, and ritual) when you are not clear about whether you should have it, you may have mixed results.

Example 1: Many have developed the habit of thinking that we can have what we need but not what we want. You may pray for a car, while not being certain of your worthiness. So if you think you don't really need the car, you may create one that does not run or one that needs repairs or has some other difficulty attached.

Example 2: You may ask for $20,000 to buy a car. You may get $20,000, and with it an unexpected expense that eats up the $20,000. It is important to be clear about what you want. Do you want money or do you want a car? Always ask for exactly what you want. Human consciousness is almost as demanding as a computer. It will normally give you exactly what you ask for, what you focus on. Doubts confuse and delay the process. So also do attempts to outline the method by which your prayer will be answered. If you try to specify where your $20,000 will come from or how it will arrive, you limit the Creator's power. And it is that power that is being (channeled) used by and through you.

Another important thing to realize is that the principle of magnetism works on your negatives as well. If you find yourself hating, even criticizing something repeatedly, that will attract the very thing that you do not want. You are using the creative aspects of the subconscious here, and it does not recognize negatives. If you say, "I don't want it to rain on my picnic," your subconscious hears, " rain on my picnic." Learn to rephrase your prayers. Pray for a clear day. Affirm that it will be clear. See the Sun shining on your picnic. Imagine how it will feel to be out in the sunshine . . . and so on.

At this point, you can begin to see the interaction between thought and a creative use of it. One must have Mercury to name, to envision, to *speak the word*. One must also understand the use of focused intent to concentrate the magnetic charge in each word, thought, or idea. Emotion may lend it power if your feelings cause you to focus more intently.

The best way to have a good life is to name/Mercury all things good/ Venus. Sun, Mercury, and Venus are pure spirit, in the form of Identity, Consciousness and Creativity. They define your spiritual self as a Being/Sun who is worthy and loved by the Creator/Venus and has been given the power to name/Mercury all of life as s/he chooses.

Venus in the Elements and Signs

Venus in Fire

Fire Venus values energy, as essence, the spark of life. S/he loves life and values all that lives because it is alive.

Aries: Aries Venus loves challenges, adventure, action. S/he has courage and ambition.

Leo: Leo Venus values heritage and/or inherited values. In some this fixed Venus is grounded to the superficial and can be snobbish. In the more evolved this is a love of the Divine Heritage which generates gratitude expressed as increased creativity. Appreciation equals attraction-of- more.

Sagittarius: Sagittarius Venus loves expansion, growth, and truth. To this end, s/he loves travel and languages because they expand horizons. She is generous to a fault. She learns to learn and loves to teach. Her goal is always wisdom, especially in the form of *higher truth*.

Venus in Earth

Earth Venus values and most easily attracts substance, especially the physical amenities of life. It treasures comfort and pleasure. These are the strongest magnetic fields of the zodiac and must be used wisely, remembering that proper evaluation is critical to a worth-while life. The more you look for good, the more good you will see. But if you look for faults, the more faults you will see.

Taurus: Taurus Venus values money and appreciation. She wants things to be nice and may become a serious people-pleaser. At some point she must realize her own worth and stop putting other people's comfort and happiness before her own. She is capable of acquiring wealth.

Virgo: Virgo Venus values order, efficiency, and good function. At some point she must realize that beauty can be more than rote order. She must learn to *stop and smell the roses* because overwork and its accompanying fatigue are inefficient.

Capricorn: Capricorn Venus values honor above all. She knows the value of maturity. Usually successful, these people are the authorized managers of life, and most are good bosses. Capricorn Venus' management style is based on praise and rewards.

Venus in Air

Air Venus values ideas, words, intelligence. Natives value communication and relationship. They also value space, needing room to *breathe*, both physically and mentally.

Gemini: Gemini Venus values parallel relationships. Preferred company is with siblings, peers, neighbors. Preferred study is elementary, logical. Some use a rating system for evaluating themselves and/or others.

Libra: Libra Venus values equality and sharing, often expressed in committed partnerships. Libra is the sign of true conversation, where equals share ideas for mutual pleasure. Her primary goal must be to realize her own worth and to prize it sufficiently to avoid relationships that lower her vibration.

Aquarius: Aquarius Venus equals impersonal and unconditional love. It values abstract relationships and communication, as with like-minded people associating in consciousness groups. Even individual relationships/friendships are relatively impersonal and elevated. The highest Aquarian values are knowledge and its capacity for change and evolution. There is a tendency to outgrow relationships as consciousness rises.

Venus in Water

Water Venus values feelings, and sometimes needs. Here, conditioning may intrude so that you attract only those things that you *need*. Note: No matter what you think that you need or want, you can only attract it into your life if you regard it as valuable and yourself as worthy of having it.

Cancer: Cancer Venus values home and family because they represent the security and/or visibility necessary for growth. Her prime value is growth, particularly its first stages, as represented by birth and emerging from the soil.

Scorpio: Scorpio Venus values passion, but must not limit its definition to a sexual one. You can draw anything that you are passionate about into your life. Be sure that your passions are really good for you.

Pisces: Pisces Venus is *master of love* and loves all without discrimination, often attracting good things casually, without thought, from a state of powerful magnetism.

The Identity Structure: Moon

The Moon in our design is the second level of identity, which can be called Daughter of Earth, and has a very different role from the Sun or the planets. It is a satellite of Earth, almost part of it, so we can think of it as related to incarnation on Earth. We might think of it by sign as the reason why a spiritual being chooses to incarnate. The Moon is strongly connected to what we do and/or the way we do it. It may or may not define your profession, but will define how you express your profession.

It has been said that we cannot look on the face of God without being blinded. Neither can we look directly at the Sun without blinding. Let the Sun represent the god-spirit, which is our spiritual parent. He is the very life energy which is our Source, but he is also the source of everyone else. Only a small portion of this energy can be contained within a human form.

The Moon then becomes our symbolic transformer, selecting the correct frequency and voltage for this lifetime. It *channels* the correct amount and type of spirit/energy for our incarnating purpose.

Another way to view this is to say that the Moon formats the Solar energy for our life manuscript. So then we may say that the Sun is Spiritual Energy and defines us as Son/Daughter of a Heavenly Father, while the Moon defines us as Son/Daughter of Mother Earth. If the Sun is God, the Moon is Goddess—the Goddess that gives birth to humanity.

Your Moon symbolizes your Soul in its function as the *silver cord* between spirit and body. It is the lens through which we look at the Deity/Spirit/Sun.

For the pre-Indigos it also symbolizes the Mother, or more accurately the mother-child bond, whose physical expression is the umbilical.

For Indigos, Crystals, and Rainbow children, the Moon may seem to represent the Father, and the Sun the Mother. This seems to be because, in them, humanity has reached a turning point.

Earlier generations were more identified with the idea of lifting the physical up to the spiritual. These *new* humans have completed that and made the shift into full awareness of their spiritual heritage and identity. They identify with the task of making spirit physical, of pouring it *down* into a human form. Their efforts are directed to fitting the spiritual identity into a physical structure and making their bodies work for them.

The Moon is related to the need system. Its domain is feelings, which communicate basic needs (water, food, space, air, protection, etc.) In the earlier generations, the need system was initially absorbed from the mother or primary caretaker through the mother-child bond. For adults this usually necessitated a complete reevaluation and redefinition of their needs in later life.

The *new humans* are born with an established need system. They know what they need and have little tolerance for unmet needs or those who try to tell them what they need. Perhaps their greatest frustration is that they come into a world that does not recognize the presence of a mature consciousness in these immature bodies.

Moon in the Elements and Signs

Moon in Fire

The Fire Moon/Soul does not so much convert Solar energy as it motivates it. It may fire up, light up, or stir up this energy, producing an electrical force that sets life in motion. It formats spirit into desire, action, or extension, warming us to relationship, heating creativity, lighting our path to the stars, to the future.

Aries: The Aries Soul burns with desire, the desire to be a visible, tangible expression of Spirit. This Moon heats up the Solar energy, causing it to reach out, sometimes creating *solar flares*. It brings forth the "I am" aspect of any Sun. If the environment does not support this, it will fight for its right to survive, particularly the survival of the Solar identity.

Leo: The Leo Soul is more stable, like a hearth fire, a lamp, or candle. The Leo Moon shapes Solar energy to action, performance, creativity. It brings out the "brightness" of the Sun, its shine, its *starring role* in our life. If circumstances try to hide the Solar light *under a bushel*[2] its energy may flare, causing the native to *act up* or *act out* in dramatic ways, making the Sun visible in whatever way it can.

Sagittarius: The Sagittarius Soul burns to expand the Solar outreach and/or expression, ever striving to become something more. Its intent is to expand the Solar potential as the *light of the world*.[3] Sagittarius' fire is enthusiasm, flaring to joy. It emphasizes the radiant quality and unquenchable spirit of the Sun. If resistance tries to dim the Sun, it may exaggerate some Solar aspect to the point of ridiculousness, producing a *larger than life* effect.

---

[2] From the bible, Mark 8:16, Luke 11:33.
[3] From the bible, Matthew 5:14.

Moon in Earth

The Earth Soul converts solar energy into substance, storing it in the structures and forms that ground our lives into reality. It concentrates energy into things of value, things for use, and symbols of accomplishment.

Taurus: The Taurus Moon converts energy into symbols of self-worth. If unhindered, it naturally produces money and other goods in an adequate-to-abundant supply. Taurus is the builder of structural integrity, using magnetic fields to bind substance into those forms considered valuable. When the early environment does not value the native or does not teach reasonable values, the Taurus Moon may channel too much Solar energy into the accumulation of wealth.

Virgo: The Virgo Moon channels energy into service, especially as focused through good function. Its first task is to keep the body healthy. Beyond that it focuses on useful work. Unhindered, it is the true efficiency expert, handling life with grace and ease. All too often this Soul is burdened with excess guilt and/or a heavy sense of duty. Carried too far, the health may be destroyed, if only to get rest for the body and quiet for the soul.

Capricorn: The Capricorn Moon is the true *Old Soul*, mature, responsible, and wise. S/he manages energy wisely, knowing how to time, arrange, and delegate, for s/he has lifetimes of experience to draw upon. From birth, these people are "old for their age" but often seem to reverse the aging process in their later years.

The great hazzard for Capricorn is that it *represents the outer limits of the current definition of humanity*. This can feel as though there were no growing room, leading to depression. Their great task is to realize that they can grow, simply by choosing to exceed the limits-of-possibility in the general consciousness. Their task is to become *more than human*, helping to expand the definition of what a spirit may do while housed in physical form.

Moon in Air

The Air Soul converts Solar energy into consciousness, specifically the type of consciousness involved in ideas, learning, and communication. Communication is a major ingredient in relationship, which may also be a focus of the Air Moon.

Gemini: The Gemini Moon is the great communicator. S/he loves to exchange information, news, ideas, even gossip. This placement often results in a double application of the Solar energy as two styles or approaches to life. One reason for this may be an excess of energy that can be best handled by doing two or more things at once. Another way to apply this duality is to find a balance between physical and mental activity. Gemini can almost be in perpetual-motion and needs to allow that to be okay. Then s/he will not have to talk so fast to explain!

Libra: The Libra Moon applies energy to sharing, especially to the sharing of information, ideas and learning. This frequently gets focused into *sharing space* as in committed unions. The Libra Moon may think she needs another to complete her, but that is a mis-perception. In fact, the Libra Moon will not be happy without someone to share with, but far too often s/he ends up doing all the giving while others do the taking. S/he must learn that true sharing only works between equals. If s/he can learn to share with the world through writing, publishing, or broadcasting, peace may come.

Because s/he *stands between*, this is often the placement of the mediator, the peacemaker, bringing opposites into balance and cooperation. In its highest application, this is the Medium—or in modern language, the Channel. This one becomes a bridge across space and time, allowing communication between the visible and invisible worlds.

Aquarius: The Aquarius Moon directs Solar energy into ever higher/wider realms of consciousness, producing unusual applications and results. This is the inspired and/or inventive (Galactic) Soul. The next step beyond Libra's mediumship, Aquarius is the Adept who channels energy into infinite variations of thought and form.

Many of these Souls never feel *at home* on Earth because they are moving beyond being *only human*. They are moving into their divinity, and/or their universality. Most are considered *rare or quirky* and some find humility useful in coping with a world that forever feels a bit alien. Sometimes this represents the last Earth incarnation of a cycle.

Moon in Water

The Water Moon channels Solar Energy fluidly. This is the basic truth of all Moons, but it is most obvious with the water Moons. At best, they provide a steady stream, naturally fulfilling needs as they occur. The Moon is most *at home* in water. In water signs, the Soul is most obviously capable of directing the *flow* of energy, channeling it to the supply of needs, as modern water systems provide water through good plumbing. Keep in mind that water naturally finds its own level and conforms to the shape of its container. However, a highly energetic Sun filtered through a water Moon can sometimes cause overflow, swamping or fog, producing fits of rage, depression or confusion.

Cancer: The Cancer Moon, the most lunar of all Moons, directs energy into birth, emergence, and growth. It channels Solar energy fluidly into bloodstreams, and wombs, and mother's milk It is a young and growing placement, needy and strongly connected to mother and/or family, often over-bonded to the point of having difficulty leaving home. Adults may base all relationships on need, being needy or needed.

At its highest, Cancer represents ongoing growth, which, reaching completion at one level, transforms into another and continues growing. *Theirs is the secret of eternal life.*

Scorpio: The Scorpio Moon stores energy in deep pools of passion. This Moon concentrates Solar energy, compressing it into ice for containment, and/or heating it to steam where it may be vented or harnessed to run engines. Intensity is its mode of operation, producing the highest creativity, the coldest manipulation, the biggest explosions. It is *force*—the force that forever clears space for tomorrow's manifestations.

Perhaps more than any other, the Scorpio Moon depends on the willpower or willingness of the Solar Energy behind it. It can sit silent, flow deep under ground, or present a steaming geyser, occasionally taking on volcanic proportions. At its best, it then resurrects, rising like a Phoenix to soar with the eagles. This may be the most powerfully creative of Souls, but traditionally the Scorpio's power has been crammed down, misused and abused. Still, we are learning to love and to use that power. It will take us to the stars and beyond. This Moon is the true Adept and/or Alchemist.

Pisces: The Pisces Moon is oceanic, deep, and tidal, and extending beyond the horizon. Within its depths may be found the sum of life's qualities. It is the all that extends beyond the reach of human senses. It is the Master Soul who has mastered needs and can often be seen magically attracting whatever s/he needs. This Moon, like the ocean, is both wide and deep, and constantly in motion. Here we see the rhythm of the tides, bringing information from its depths, up to the light of day.

It is tender-hearted and easily wounded, but equally easy to heal. The problem and the glory of the Master Soul is that, like the ocean, its limits are beyond our ability to perceive. These natives are mystical and magical, often beyond the understanding of logic-bound younger souls. They can be a delight and/or a frustration, as wonderful and as terrible as the ocean.

Earth/Ascendant

For purposes of our design, we include the Earth[4] with the Moon, and use the Ascendant for its symbol. It is a product of pouring Solar Energy through a lunar transformer/channel into a physical form, a physical life.

The way we learn to see and name ourselves comes from the time and place of our birth, which we use the Ascendant to signify. Together with the first house, it describes what we are likely to see in the mirror, as learned from the *names* we are called—the habitual descriptive terms used by our immediate family. It is self-image, meaning what we think that we *look like* and project outward as a persona.

Your Ascendant is how you identify for this incarnation, the impression you make, the most visible part of you. Symbolically, it is derived from pouring the Sun's energy through the Moon's outline for this life. It is what the outcome *looks like*.

By sign, the Ascendant describes the outer portion of our visible expression on Earth. That expression makes us sufficiently *solid* and substantial to accomplish our incarnational intent. It gives form to what would otherwise be transparent. It provides sufficient substance for handling a solid reality. It is the difference between being a *ghost* and a human.

Realistically, the entire wheel of the horoscope shows the (metaphysical) body and lifestyle, but the Ascendant is the side we turn to the world.

Up to this point the astrological Kabala describes the *creation* of a being. It shows what *goes into* making us who we are. The remainder of the design will show how we use and express what

---

[4]Some horoscopes show a symbol for the Earth. What we give here does not refer to that. It uses Earth as a symbol for the Ascendant, simply because incarnation on Earth is necessary to create the wheel of a chart, and the Ascendant is the most visible part of the incarnational image.

has been given us. As we are created, so we will create. As we have received, so we will give—through the remaining planets, beginning with Mars.

Ascendant in the Elements and Signs

Ascendant in Fire

A fire Ascendant looks active, energetic, motivated. It acts in its own self-interest, as a light bearer or a way shower.

Aries: Aries rising *looks like* a Survivor and/or a Warrior, powered from his/her own center. There is an instinctive knowledge of existence as the *prime directive*. At higher levels, Aries is a Pioneer or Seed-being. At worst s/he is paranoid.

Leo: Leo rising first *looks like* a Performer. Energy is poured into specific roles, inherited from a *Heavenly Father* or an Earthly one. S/he is the star in his or her own life, in society, or in the Universe. At best s/he lights up life. At worst s/he loses his or her identity/Sun, pouring energy into empty shells, pretending that s/he is the role.

Sagittarius: Sagittarius rising *looks like* a Traveler or a Teacher, forever pushing the horizons of experience or knowledge for Self and/or Others. At best s/he is a disseminator of information. At worst, s/he is an abandoned child, running from life, afraid to venture far from the beliefs that sustain his or her will to live. In whatever expression, Sagittarius is a bit *bigger than life*.

Ascendant in Earth

Earth Ascendants look solid, visible, grounded. They appear *down to earth*, practical, and substance oriented. These individuals may appear to ignore their Sun and/or Moon. Instead, the Sun and Moon are integrated into, harnessed as, or managed by the Ascendant.

Taurus: Taurus rising looks good, seems pleasant and accommodating, and is often a people-pleaser. The native appears to be a valuable asset to others. At its worst, Taurus produces a self-image as *The Owned* or *The Owner*. At its best, Taurus Rising represents a full integration of Soul, Spirit, and Body, as one knowing s/he is worthy to have the best in life. The integrity of intake and outreach will be so balanced as to manifest the ability to *feed the economy*.

Virgo: Virgo rising looks *functional*, and/or *useful*—healthy and/or employable. This placement sometimes leads to a self-image as User or Used, with guilt overworking body and/or soul until health issues intervene, providing rest. At its best, Sun and Moon work together efficiently to produce useful goods and/or services. It then represents *conscious perfection*—the awareness that *you are the perfect you*, entitled to use your life as you will. Doing this, you function from your pre-incarnational intention and your life works smoothly, easily, efficiently, and productively.

Capricorn: Capricorn rising *looks responsible, mature*. Young Capricorns often appear older than their chronological age. This one *looks like* an elder sibling, and often is in the birth family.

The self-image manages the entire chart, as an agent of Sun and Moon. This is the highest version of a fully grounded self-image. It is one that has evolved over lifetimes. In this lifetime it reaches its limits insofar as the native accepts the definition of the word *human* in the general consciousness. It cannot evolve much further without moving or exceeding those limitations.

The reality this symbolizes is that of spiritual maturity. Look to the remainder of the chart for information on whether the native will manage his/her life within those limits, push them outward or overcome or break them.

At best this represents one honored and honorable. At worst it leads to over-work and depression. The key is this: You are designed to be responsible for yourself, your own choices and decisions. You are responsible for managing your own energies and abilities and for your own protection and defense. Your most important lesson is that you are *not* responsible for any other adult, including your own adult offspring!

Ascendant in Air

Air Ascendants *look like* they need space, because they are reflective. To have an object and a reflection, space is required. In this world an object and its reflection create a relationship. These individuals look *related* to others, in one way or another, and the relationships are defined by the space in them.

Gemini: Gemini rising often presents a *double self-image*. These people are frequently called *little brother, big sister,* or *one of the Jones twins* during childhood. The relationship is a parallel one in which two people are seen or spoken of as one. If they do not learn to manage or integrate the two images, the result can be a bi-polar or two-faced appearance in the adult.

Some seem *tethered* to their family, limited to *short journeys*, unable to get far from home. Some talk or study compulsively, while others give up, go silent, and/or bury themselves in mathematics or some other strictly logical study.

Rising Geminis look intelligent. Many have *encyclopedic* data bases in their brains from a lifetime of information gathering. Others become avid gossips. Intended for both learning and communication, Gemini may mature well to become a knowledgeable writer, speaker, or teacher.

Libra: Libra Rising is marked by the family as *The Other*, appearing or actually looking different from other siblings, sometimes different from the entire family. Occasionally, this is from being *the only girl*, or the only one who struggles in school, or the only one who keeps a neat room. Most often there is more to the story because they usually struggle to *fit in*, often driving much of their real identity underground.

Another expression is that of becoming a *partner* to one parent in a parental power struggle. These people grow up feeling that they must have an *other half*, a partner or mate to complete them. It can feel like having half of a self-image.

The real meaning of Libra rising is *committed*, and historically natives have lived in societies that seldom considered any commitment other than the marriage partnership. Partnerships require equality to work well, and many Libras grow up without experiencing equal relationships. Their personal evolution may then involve serial monogamy before they realize their true commitment to their own inner partner.

At worst, Libra will lose the Self in a bond that s/he cannot or will-not break, with spirit broken-to-harness, a sacrifice on the altar of some religious dogma. At its best, Libra rising recognizes an impersonal commitment to act as a mediator or a spiritual commitment that allows development of an innate talent for mediumship (channeling).

Aquarius: Aquarius rising looks *different*, sometimes appearing to be in the wrong family, even on the wrong planet. Many have the look of an Adept. As we near the next age, increasing numbers are almost transparent, psychically and sometimes physically.

Mundanely, they are often *ignored children*, living on hopes and wishes. This may be lonely, but its grace is that it does not force sufficient behavior changes to harm the innate spirit.

The sign Aquarius is just beyond the generally-accepted human limits of Capricorn, *thus more-than-human*. When it rises, the aura is clearer or whiter than most, creating an impression of looking quite unusual. In a world that often fears or hates anything different, their transparency, their ability to *fade into the woodwork*, can be a great gift.

Some *look crazy*, but seldom are. The least-evolved version of this placement clowns its way through life. The more serious become vehicles through which universal knowledge is poured into humanity. Seemingly *from the future*, genius is common and versatility is a given.

As we move deeper into the twenty-first century, increasing numbers of these natives are born knowing who and why they are. Possibility People, they appear to live between the worlds. Whether ordained or not, they are natural priest/esses, who inspire others.

Ascendant in Water

Water Ascendants look emotional and/or needy. Feelings are *the mind of the body*, intended to communicate needs. These individuals see themselves as or through their feelings. They may feel the need of others in their lives, from a feeling that being with another provides the containment they need to prevent being *soaked up*, *drained away*, or *evaporated*.

Cancer: Cancer Ascendants look dependent, and may be called *baby*. Females are said to *look like* their mothers and to be as dependent (or not), as she seems to be. Males are more likely to remain dependent on their mothers—sometimes called a *mama's boy*.

Scorpio: Scorpio Ascendants look powerful. This is quite problematic because, historically, the only way most parents recognized power was in the form of blame. These are passionate beings who seem intense. All too often their passion and power are feared and hated by others who blame them—especially blaming them for their own abusive behavior. ("You made me do it.")

The Identity Structure: Moon

The Identity Structure: Mars

A t the top-center of our chart is the Sun, our Spiritual Identity. Next comes the Moon, our Soul—the transformer which fits Spiritual Energy into Physical Form. Next comes the Ascendant, gateway to the chart-wheel, which shows the environmental structure for this lifetime. Spirit has become Incarnate form.

Each of us is an image or reflection of All-That-Is, the Whole (Holy) Spirit which is the energy-essence that underlies and inhabits creation and It's Offspring—otherwise known as individual Humans. As our Divine Antecedent radiates, even so do we. Mars becomes our Human Identity, including the impulse to radiate energy (love and light). It is the element that reaches for our desires and/or the outreach to Life, to Others, the Universe, to All-That-Is.

Martian outreach is initially expressed through the Human forms of Mercury (learning) and Venus (relating), which can now be expressed through Chiron and Eris.

Light/Intelligence is further expressed as Expansion/Jupiter, and Love/Creation is further facilitated as Contraction/Saturn or concentration of energy through boundaries, limits, and definitions as used to contain and condense energy into form.

In our Kabbalah, we make Mars part of the Identity structure. Mars represents the Son aspect of any trinity. As the sign Leo refers to Son of God, so Aries refers to Son of Man. Mars identifies us as incarnate spirit, the result of expressing divinity in human form, the visible expression of invisible spirit.

Life is that which moves, grows, changes, becomes. Stagnation is the beginning of death. Mars is the energy that drives living systems. He loves life. He wants to live. When Mars-energy evolves into a pioneering spirit, it does so from the desire to preserve life for others, and for the future. At any time when the quantity or quality of life begins to decline, some Martian spirit will establish new colonies where life will be free to express fully. When human evolution slows, Martian Seed Beings sow the ideas which set it moving again.

The clearest expression of Mars is outreach. It is humanity reaching out. Its connection with desire is the association with reaching out for what we want and the first thing Mars wants is to live. The second is to live as himself, true to his own spirit. It is the planet of Incarnation and Individuation.

Mars-ruled beings have a sense of connection that goes beyond relationship. For them, *I* means all that is connected to me, and the entire world may be included in that. The Son of Man is he who knows himself as a holographic being, a portion of the All which contains all. He sees no need to unite what was never divided.

Mars represents the way we reach out for life, and for whatever makes life better. It also describes the way we reach out to others. The Mars/Aries spirit is sometimes called selfish, but is more accurately *centered in the Self*. Mars knows, better than any other planet, that each individual is the center of his or her own universe.

As the *survival instinct*, Mars represents the knowledge that human life is the highest value in existence. Without humanity, any God/dess who still existed would be meaningless.

Mars has suffered long from religions that would deny humanity its desires. So often faith is limited by the dogma that we are entitled to what we *need*, but not what we *want*. What we now call *poverty consciousness* is rooted in this betrayal. In reality, needs are physical and desires are spiritual. Mars is a fire/spiritual planet. Desire represents our spiritual needs, those things we reach out for in the attempt to move ourselves beyond mere existence to that *life and greater life*, spoken of by Jesus ben Joseph.

At another level Mars represents the energy you have beyond what is required to maintain your physical beingness. It is that drive that urges us to be more, to do more, to accomplish something of value.

The sign in which Mars resides tells us something about what we want—meaning what our spirit needs. It also suggests the way we reach for life and what we most want out of life.

Mars in the Elements and Signs

Mars in Fire

Mars is at home in fire signs, being a rather fiery planet. Here the outreach is pure and clear as Mars reaches out for Existence/Aries, Expression/Leo, and Expansion/Sagittarius—the primary components of ongoing Life.

Aries: Aries Mars is pure survivalist, one who is fighting for life. His life lesson is to realize that his survival is a given. He may then use that energy to power pioneering projects.

Leo: Leo Mars is active and dramatic. This Mars reaches out for a role that will fulfill the desires of his heart. If thwarted or misunderstood, he may rage.

Sagittarius: Sagittarius Mars reaches for the stars, forever extending and expanding consciousness from a great thirst for *more*. He is hungry for truth.

Mars in Earth

Mars in earth is magnetic by nature. His *outreach* is more a matter of drawing desires to him than of reaching for them. Dogged, stubborn, and determined, he draws things of Value/Taurus, things of Usefulness/Virgo, and things that are Honorable/Capricorn.

Taurus: Taurus Mars reaches for/attracts substance, especially for money and goods. He preserves his survival by storing up for the future.

Virgo: Virgo Mars reaches for/attracts a healthy life style. His mode of action is service, so he becomes the efficiency expert who makes every motion work for him. His spiritual goal is to learn how to serve without stress, doing the things his heart most desires to do.

Capricorn: Capricorn Mars has mature desires and outreach. He is a natural manager and knows how to distribute energies or tasks in order to accomplish the maximum. His great desire in life is for success for himself and others.

Mars in Air

Mars in air is space-conscious, a bridge-personality. He reaches out for information and/or relationship. More polarized than other elemental placements, this Mars is very conscious of the need to reach out across space and/or time.

Gemini: Gemini Mars reaches for the nearby, the elementary, using *names*/words. The theme of his life is "Name it and claim it."

Libra: Libra Mars reaches out for the opposite or complimentary, contrasting self with not-self. This Mars may struggle with altruism, trying to give to others all that he wants for himself.

His lesson is to realize that whatever he does for himself, first, will automatically be the best for others.

Aquarius: Aquarius Mars is Universal Outreach. Here, he is most adventurous, reaching out across wider spaces and greater time, seeking the new and different in invention and inspiration. He is the great Changer of life, empowering changes for the future.

Mars in Water

Mars in water can be energy in flow or it can be *soggy*. When emotion is used to drive us, it works well. When it is used to manipulate others, the *tide* may come in and overwhelm us.

Cancer: Cancer Mars grows, and hopefully outgrows childish ways. It must *grow up*. It must learn to dry its tears, and take action.

Scorpio: Scorpio Mars is an engine, powering creation in positive or negative ways, depending on the emotion applied. Tempted to manipulate others, it must let go and allow spirit to work through its living form. When *willingness* replaces *willpower*, there is no limit to the magic that can happen.

Pisces: Pisces Mars is Cosmic Outreach. It is almost desireless, a state derived from the kind of Mastery that provides all possible needs and desires in spontaneous ways. Here it becomes the simple flow of undifferentiated Life, fulfilling Itself. It should be trusted—taken for granted, to serve us best.

Personalized Consciousness: Chiron

Human outreach/Mars, through our roles as Son/Daughter of Man, takes four basic forms: Chiron, Eris, Jupiter and Saturn. Chiron is Yang and represents the multi-level aspect of Human Consciousness. Eris is Yin and intended to reflect Human creativity and goodness.

Life on Earth is dualistic and may be symbolized by respiration or tidal motion. In the process of life we alternate between pushing our limits and contracting energy into form. That duality is represented by Expansion/Jupiter and Contraction/Saturn.

We may think of Mercury as representing generic consciousness or innate intelligence. This is personalized by filtering it through the personal consciousness structure, from Mercury through Chiron, Jupiter and Neptune. We might say that Mercury perceives information, Chiron digests it, Jupiter uses it for growth, and Neptune stores the results outside the realms of ordinary awareness, in the impersonal sub- and super- consciousness ranges of memory.

The discovery of Chiron in 1977 symbolized a maturation point for humanity, and heralded the birth of a new evolutionary level in humanity. *The New Kids*[5] are incarnating with much wider perceptual ranges, and much better memory-access than was common in earlier generations. In them, the limits of visible information began to overlap that which had been invisible to earlier generations, as the general consciousness began its final rise toward the Age of Aquarius.

Around this time, information systems came to our attention and the increasing use of personal computers provided a symbol for what was happening in the general consciousness. In the years that followed, the World Wide Web came into general use almost simultaneously with increased attention to the extension of human minds into the Neptunian ranges of Universal Intelligence/Akashic Records. The overall function of Chiron is to be the symbolic Facilitator of the consciousness-rise which accompanies each new maturation-level, in individuals and in the general population. In practice, Chiron is the modem between, and the file-handler for, both individual and Universal consciousness.

Consciousness Structure/Chiron-Mercury

Like Mercury, Chiron has multiple duties. Interestingly, Chiron was not found at the outer limits of the known solar system, as were previous new planetary discoveries. Instead, this major asteroid or minor planet was found in a highly elliptical orbit that crosses between Saturn and Uranus. It can be noted that Chiron provides a *bridge* between the social planets (those between Earth and Uranus) and the impersonal *galactic ambassadors* (Uranus, Neptune, Pluto).

Chiron also symbolizes the link between the outer senses and the inner ones, symbolically connecting Mercury and Jupiter to Neptune. Chiron is an information *handler*, ushering in knowl-

---

[5]Indigos, followed by Crystals, with Rainbows yet to come.

edge that gives us more control of our lives through a better understanding of how human consciousness works, especially the creative aspects of it.

In practical terms, Chiron cn be regarded as the keeper of the memory files. Chiron's domain includes the awareness that even forgotten knowledge is not gone. As we become increasingly familiar with the dynamics of our internal information systems, we learn to access memories from the past and future incarnations of self and others. Perhaps more importantly, we begin to understand the difference between our innate levels of awareness and the conditioning superimposed upon us early in life. In so doing we retrieve (sometimes buried) information about who, what, and how we truly are.

Ultimately, Chiron is facilitating the conscious union of spirit and body. In the process, much healing occurs, for *DIS-EASE* is ever rooted in a misaligned spirit-body connection. On a more mundane level, the misalignment is between our conditioning and our essential nature. What we *think that we know* rubs against what we inherently know, causing friction and stress.

Chiron represents the use we make of our innate intelligence (capacity for conscious awareness), especially the way we use it to facilitate personal growth. As toddlers we memorize words. As schoolchildren we memorize ideas, especially about how the world works. In time we may also memorize ideals and/or beliefs. Mercury records data. Chiron handles Mercury files, and includes the capacity to make much more information accessible to us than was once believed possible.

Memory files must be organized properly for efficient use. As we age, periodically we must reorganize these memory files. The no-nos of early childhood become may-dos/can-dos as we mature. Much that is forbidden before adolescence becomes mandated by society after it. At every significant maturation point (examples: ages 15, 21, 30, 40, 50, and 60) some reorganization occurs. This *file-handling* is a function of Chiron as information is sorted and resorted for efficiency in handling the various phases of life.

Chiron files experience for future reference. It initially represents conscious memory as applied to daily choices and practical living skills. A good filing system for memory is the key to organizing our lives efficiently and to handling the activities and events called living.

Mercury/Learning is natural to humanity. Notice the eagerness to learn and communicate, in any small child. Chiron's files are accumulated as the child practices the art of living successfully. Gradually s/he learns how to get needs met, what gets approval, what feels good, what hurts, etc. The information is stored in memory.

Memories are stored in many layers. The top layer is Chiron's immediate domain, for it contains information about those things we deal with on a daily basis. The most useful lessons of life must be within easy reach. Periodic rearrangement, allowing some information to recede and be superceded by other files, is necessary. Mercury may have been adequate for the simple tasks of childhood, but by adolescence we must begin to apply what we have learned to the task of independent living. This is Chiron's domain.

As the years pass, with the expansion of consciousness, we need Chiron to act as a search engine for our greater accumulation of information. The *absent-minded* person may have problems with his or her filing system, due to some family dysfunction that interferes with logical processing. Then Chiron may need to call on his healing abilities to repair Soul wounds.

For seekers, Chiron takes on yet another task. As human consciousness reaches toward the vast realms of Neptune, Chiron transforms into a modem. A primary difference between older and younger generations is the degree of Chiron activation. When the senses expand sufficiently, we need ways to call up the contents of universal memory. Chiron provides the link that, when we mature to a point of readiness, allows us to explore across time and space. Evolving from simple file-handling to search engine, Chiron allows the human mind to surf the *universal web.*[6]

The sign placement (and aspects) of Chiron symbolize how we use what we learn, the quality of memory retrieval, and the capacity to access deeper and higher realms of consciousness.

Chiron in the Elements and Signs

Chiron in Fire

Chiron in fire is designed to facilitate self-awareness, creativity, and consciousness-expansion.

Aries: In Aries, files are sorted for survival. When survival issues become too compulsive, Chiron reminds us that our lives cannot be taken without our permission.

Leo: In Leo, files are sorted for/by role, and Chiron's most important task is to remind us that a role is not an identity. Roles can and do change. He also reminds us that our heritage is equally human and divine.

Sagittarius: In Sagittarius, files are sorted for reasonableness. Information *must make sense.* Chiron's major task becomes a search for Truth. In Sagittarius, Chiron facilitates conceptual thinking and the use of principles and applications, of concepts and symbols. Here his service as a link between logic and intuition is most apparent, often producing the Conscious Channel—one who blends logical and intuitive functions automatically in speech and/or writing.

Chiron in Earth

Chiron in Earth is designed to facilitate self-worth, conscious

---

[6]Akashic Record or Universal Consciousness—the vast MIND that enco mpasses all minds.

efficacy, and successful living. It is very grounded and practical, so the filing system is especially designed for physical well-being.

Taurus: In Taurus, memories are sorted for value. Chiron may remind us that values are subjective and relative to our own nature and purpose. He further reminds us that it is difficult to create what has no personal value.

Virgo: In Virgo, memories are sorted for usefulness. Chiron reminds us that use is related to context, and may depend on our innate purpose and level of maturity. What is useless to a child may be useful to an adult, and vice versa. In Virgo, Chiron's greatest task may be the development of a healthy ego able to serve our incarnational purpose.

Capricorn: In Capricorn, Chiron becomes a true memory-manager. Here sorting has reached an apex of usefulness that leads to honor and success. Still, Chiron reminds us that these are very subjective terms and must be defined in personally meaningful ways. Capricorn is the gateway to a major redefinition of human purpose.

Chiron in Air

Chiron in Air is designed to facilitate awareness of the nature of and purpose for human consciousness. It encourages the accurate use of language and correct naming.

Gemini: In Gemini, Chiron is learning about the (identical) twin-ship of the logical-left and intuitive-right brain function. Intuition *is* logic, functioning at the speed of light. There is no either-or choice. They are the twin faces of one function.

Here the focus is on a parallel relationship that functions hand-in-hand, almost undifferentiated, and neither complete without the other. Although conditioning may interfere, creating malfunctions like dyslexia, always Chiron in Gemini continues to question, to seek. In doing so, answers come.[7] Chiron becomes a bridge that allows the translation of information from imagery to language, from the unnamed to the named.

Libra: Chiron in Libra is about creating the conscious union between logic and intuition that permits true mediumship. It is about a unified and bonded team in which neither logic nor intuition is allowed to dominate or control the other. Logic and intuition share the tasks of awareness and creativity.

Somewhat less blended than Gemini Chiron, childhood conditioning of Libra Chiron can lead to arguments between logic and intuition until the individual finds an efficient way to marry them. This may call for certain *ritual* practices (usually forms of self-hypnosis) to facilitate the connection. It matters not how the union is formed/activated, only that it leads to an easy shift from *conscious knowledge* to sub- or super-conscious knowledge, channeled-through communication. This placement marks the true medium (channel), able to facilitate communication between the visible and invisible worlds.

Aquarius: Like Chiron, Aquarius is a bridge. It is the *galactic* bridge between Earth and the Cosmos. Chiron in Aquarius is an advanced placement, one that *stands between the worlds*, functioning at a higher evolutionary state than is generally believed possible. Because it functions above the traditional human range, it leads to a kind of transparency that can make natives nearly invisible. Consequently, most format this to provide *sudden inspiration*—flashes of enlightenment or invention. This placement facilitates great *leaps of knowledge*, information that may seem to come from the distant realms of time or space.

Aquarius Chiron may be a bit uncomfortable for some, because its function is so different from existing evolutionary states that it is sometimes regarded as insanity. In fact, it simply represents an application of consciousness that is far ahead of its (Earthly)

---

[7]Image train-tracks, coming together in the distance.

time, and/or outside the general consciousness. This is a *more-than-man* placement, because it functions at a higher frequency than the general population.

Chiron in Water

Water signs are generally though of as *unconscious*. Chiron in water becomes unconscious memories and a kind of automatic or organic type of information processing.

Cancer: Cancer is the *newborn* sign, so Chiron in Cancer refers to the memory files from past lives, *forgotten* at birth. Actually, these are set aside to make room for the assimilation of new experience associated with the present incarnation. Memories, abilities, and talents from earlier incarnations exist as a feeling-residue and may surface gradually as natives mature.

Scorpio: Chiron in Scorpio deals with suppressed memories and the power they hold over our lives. This placement can lead to addictions used to handle the body stresses generated by this suppression. Because it requires that we recognize the power that such secrets have, it becomes the vehicle for *handling* our transformation processes. The release of information *held hostage* becomes a great source of creative/magical power.

Pisces: Chiron in Pisces is a *master* placement. It deals with *the unknown* or the *forgotten* elements of memory, reminding us that things mastered will function automatically, without attention. This includes the files of the autonomic nervous system—such as the processes of learning to speak and to walk. We did learn these, but seldom have the capacity to retrieve the experience of doing so. Finally, it refers to things never consciously known in a personal way—the kind of files that can be *picked up* psychically.

Pisces Chiron provides automatic access to the deepest and highest recesses of awareness, in much the way that an internal modem gives our personal computer access to the World Wide

Web. It is our internal link to the Cosmic Web, otherwise called Universal Mind or Akashic Record. Because full access can lead to overwhelm, it is presently necessary for many natives to use some type of divination, like tarot, pendulums, or I Ching for focus. Alternatives are hypnotic techniques. Any of these can be used in the same way that we use ISP[8] connections for our personal computers. They channel and direct the flow of information, preventing *flooding*.

For the New Kids, born in recent years, Pisces Chiron often confers relatively easy access to past and future lives.

---

[8]Internet Service Provider.

Personalized Consciousness: Chiron

Healing for Humanity's Future: Eris

The design of the Tree of Life continues through the incarnational expression of the Life Horoscope. Beginning with Mars as the Incarnational Identity, we see how human energy is channeled through Human Consciousness on the left and Human Creativity on the right under the auspices of Virgo and Libra.

Light/Mercury and Love/Venus are equal and united emanations of Spirit/Sun. However, when Spirit incarnates into Human form, duality is a necessity at the beginning of the journey to self-awareness. The recognition of Self starts with logical process. Logic is based on contrast and comparison. Primitive logic separates Yang and Yin, Spirit and Form, masculine assertiveness and feminine magnetism. It then adds judgment, making one side more valuable, more desirable, than the other. This brings us to Libra, *the other*, separating human consciousness from its mirror, Spiritual consciousness, leaving Yang and Yin out-of-balance.

Wisdom/intelligence must accept Beauty/creativity as an equal partner in life. Females must claim equality and males must accept it. Active and passive must join hands. Union must merge into unity. Humanity must reclaim its divinity.

Today, the re-balancing process has begun, but still has far to go. The feminine is still struggling with the masculine for equality. Traditional Venus is no longer adequate for the task. Early in the new millennium, a new planet was *born*/discovered, to symbolize the reuniting of Spirit and Form. Eris' task will be the healing of the all-human soul wound, returning conscious equality to the Libra areas of life.

Mythology suggests that Eris has little patience with judgments based on gender and/or brain dominance. During the 1970s, as Pluto transited Libra, a still unconscious Eris was moving across the second decanate of Aries and divorce became almost as common as marriage.

Reflecting the ancient myth of Eris, mates were often selected for physical appearance. All too often, *chemistry* took the place of reason and real compatibility *went out the window*. Marital unions were no longer valid contracts or equal partnerships. Sharing had been lost and buried under beliefs that dictated male and female roles and give-and-take relationships.

Eris Arrives

Eris' first sighting occurred on January 5, 2005. She seemed to stir up controversy, as her discovery was soon followed by an argument among the community of astronomers who suddenly decided to redefine the word *planet*. It got hot and heavy, when Pluto was downgraded and one or two asteroids were upgraded to *minor planets*. For the most part, astrologers either laughed or ignored them.

A further complication: the new planet was first named for a fictional warrior princess, Xena, but the name did not last. More observation and deeper thought renamed the new planet Eris.

Goddess of Chaos, Discord, and Laughter. Ultimately, she is here to tell us that, contrary to the religious, spiritual and theological dogmas of the past, *We Are Free.* Humanity is neither flawed, spiritually blocked, nor sinful. It was all our own doing, and because it was, it will be overcome, outgrown, or avoided when we finally decide to do so.

Introducing Eris

Eris is the new Eve, leading us to the next phase of conscious development. Eve ate the apple, fruit of the tree of *the knowledge of good and evil.* Contrast and comparison were born. Logic entered the world and humanity began the process of developing a truly human consciousness.

For her part in it, Eve was evicted from Eden, the cradle of humanity, lest she eat of the fruit of the *tree of eternal life*. It would be a long time before humans were ready for that.

After her departure from Earth in ancient times, today Eris is said to have returned to humanity because humans are now socially, emotionally, and intellectually capable of growing up and learning how to live in the world. In spite of the often-chaotic nature of such major change, it is clear that our youngest generations are arriving with a degree of spiritual maturity never before seen in whole generations. It would seem that humanity's *psychic development* is nearing completion. Eris' time has come, and she reminds us that we are truly *made in the image of our God.*

Eris knows that, even so, the realization process will be a long one, for her orbit lies far beyond that of the first eleven planets. Because it does, it will take more than 500 years for Eris to complete a full orbit and the current transiting cycle of her mission. Having begun her journey through Aries in 1922, she will not even begin to venture into Taurus until 2044.

Eris in Aries

Aries is ever the place where new abilities are first *seeded* into human consciousness, and where change first confronts stasis. Eris' influence in Aries will often resemble a battle for truth, and sometimes her methods are passive-aggressive. Still, like her brother Mars, she never gives up.

Remember the Aries nature, which resembles a small boy, climbing over all of life's rocks, through its mud puddles, and skinning his knees, but ever *keeping on keeping on.* And because of that nature, Aries overcomes difficulties that other signs refuse to tackle. We may rest assured that Eris is here to stay, for she is willing to travel such a path. She will persist and endure, for as long as it takes. Meanwhile, she is not going anywhere!

Eris in Taurus

With a number of *toe-dipping* events, Eris will gradually move into Taurus during the 2040s and 2050s. At that time her stubborn will-to-survive will be strong, and her image will become more solid, more accepted and recognized. By the beginning of the Age of Aquarius (by my estimate about 2080) her goodness—her positive aspects—will begin to emerge into human consciousness. Although not fully accepted as a ruler for Libra yet, her influence there will begin to be recognized as permanent and positive.

Eris for the Future

Know that, in the coming centuries, Eris will be struggling to bring out the best qualities of Libra to humanity. These include equality, balance, unity, harmony, and peace. Her task is to teach us that our true nature is spiritual, even when manifest in form.

Meanwhile, as of this date in 2014, in my work as a consulting astrologer, I have come across two strong, individualistic Libras. Clearly they are demonstrating the first *seeding* of the new Libra type. Remember that, like Aries, Cancer, and Capricorn, Libra is a cardinal sign. Eris will help us to remember that.

Healing for Humanity's Future: Eris

Expanding Consciousness: Jupiter

Life on Earth is dualistic and may be symbolized by respiration or tidal motion. In the process of life, we alternate between pushing our limits and contracting energy into form. That duality is represented by Expansion/Jupiter and Contraction/Saturn. Jupiter ever pushes Saturn outward, while Saturn provides safe limits for growth. Their periodic conjunctions show us when to take the next step upward or outward.

Jupiter's principle is the principle of expansion. His ultimate task is to expand our horizons and our consciousness. His energy is exponential. It is growth energy.

A primary Jupiter function is to *figure things out*. Jupiter is the processing unit of our internal computer. We use it to calculate conclusions from available data. Jupiter uses principles and concepts to postulate consequences, growth, and other outcomes. Bidirectional, it can also calculate principles from applications and consequences. Astrology is an excellent example of a Jupiterian function. Knowing the nature of the signs, planets, and houses, we may calculate a great deal about the person, thing, or event for which a horoscope is drawn.

This same function allows us to calculate the past and probable future from the present. Focused through astrology, Jupiter allows us to assess the psychological foundations of life, as an aid to greater emotional and physical health, as well as the potential outcome of increased self-awareness.

Mathematical aptitude may be from Mercury, but skill in its use is Jupiterian. However, if Chiron's memory is faulty, the skill may not be usable and Jupiter's intent to expand our knowledge base, our awareness, may be hindered. We are accustomed to thinking of humanity as divided into classes based on Jupiterian Reason or Neptunian Intuition. However, when the two join hands through Chiron, conscious mastery emerges.

A good Jupiter function allows us to predict the consequences of our actions. Again, it depends on whether we have learned and remembered what works and what does not. The signs and aspects among the four planets of consciousness can reveal much of how our internal information systems function. With the help of Neptune, a skilled Jupiterian can see beyond the obvious, beyond the aspects, noticing *wiring systems* that sometimes use other factors to bypass standard patterns in original ways.

Jupiter is generally positive, in any aspect configuration. Only in its rulership of philosophies and religions can it limit growth or do harm. It's only negative application is when Jupiterian expansion is blocked by some inherited/enforced belief system that denies our spiritual heritage as living, growing, conscious beings. When we are conditioned to believe certain things without question—notice the opposition of Gemini/questions and Sagittarius/Answers—we may avoid or delay asking the questions necessary to expand our belief systems. Even then, Jupiter's natural tendency to outgrow its limits often overcomes restrictions imposed by rigid belief systems.

Jupiter also teaches creativity. Today we are learning to reverse the adage, "I will believe it when I see it" to "I will see it when I believe it." The latter is the principle that creates the future.

Jupiter has always been optimistic and its energy output as enthusiasm (especially when combined with Mars) may be the most potent energy available to humanity. Even as we are confronted with the results of our negative beliefs, so we may also begin to exercise the power of positive beliefs. Jupiter only asks that we make the new beliefs open-ended, free to grow into a (Neptunian) potential for mastery that we may not yet understand.

This brings us to another fine Jupiterian word, *understanding*. The greatest understanding of life is that it is an ongoing creation. Every aspect of life grows, constantly and continually. There is no limitation in life that cannot be outgrown. Even truth is not absolute.

Once it was true that man could not fly. Today it is true that anyone can fly with an appropriate vehicle. For some people today, and all people at some point in the future, astral travel will become the norm. With the metaphysical author, Thomas Troward, we predict that, in time, it will even provide the key to colonizing the universe.

Jupiter in the Elements and Signs

Jupiter in Fire

Jupiter in Fire is at home, radiating both light and warmth. On the move, this Jupiter naturally, even automatically, expands horizons and/or consciousness.

Aries: Aries Jupiter is pure, joyous enthusiasm, taking natives far, expanding horizons in all directions—sometimes simultaneously!

Leo: Jupiter in Leo is meant to radiate, to *expand the light*. It can bring fame. Sometimes it overheats or blinds others. It may be proud, narcistic, dramatic, and pleasure-seeking. Its great weakness is *inherited beliefs* which can often make (family) pride an issue.

Sagittarius: Jupiter in Sagittarius is often *on the run*. Usually it runs toward. Sagittarius Jupiter is ever on a quest for *truth and greater truth*. When it is driven to run away, it is important that there be no judgment on that. When your life, or your identity, is in danger, the *only* intelligent thing to do is to run! Whether drawn or driven, internal and/or external horizons *will* expand around Jupiter.

Jupiter in Earth

Jupiter in earth refers to structural or structured expansion. Here, growth-energy is invested in form, more as creation than procreation.

Taurus: Jupiter in Taurus is about the value of beliefs. S/he figures out or understands ways to build structures of value, especially wealth.

Virgo: Jupiter in Virgo is about the use and function of beliefs. S/he handles life with skill and understanding while continually expanding his/her service. This can lead to overwork, or to wealth, depending on the remainder of the chart.

Capricorn: Jupiter in Capricorn is fully matured, showing the wisdom of the times. A good manager of time and energy, this Jupiter has a personal concept of success, believes in it, and becomes the living proof of his/her beliefs.

Jupiter in Air

Jupiter in air is almost as comfortable as it is in fire. Almost greedy for communication, it naturally believes in the power of words.

Gemini: Gemini Jupiter is youthful, studious, a collector of facts and ideas. Although, without other chart assistance, Gemini is not deep, this Jupiter can become an ever-expanding encyclopedia of information.

Libra: Libra Jupiter is altruistic and always plays fair. S/he is a great conversationalist, usually with great understanding of others, and eager to share. His/her belief in union can manifest as a compulsion to marry, and/or it may be directed toward the inner marriage of mind and spirit.

Aquarius: Aquarius Jupiter is a futurist and a natural troubleshooter. S/he uses Aquarius inspiration for Jupiter problem-solving. This Jupiter has the innate capacity to calculate conclusions from combined external, internal, and eternal data. Most have some gift of prophecy.

Jupiter in Water

Jupiter in water *feels* its way through, rather than by figuring things out in the traditional way. Most can "walk in the dark," whether it is the darkness that comes from lack of light or lack of enlightenment.

Cancer: With Jupiter in Cancer, solutions may gestate, then emerge as newborn ideas. One method is to pose a question before going to sleep. The answer will emerge in the morning.

Scorpio: Scorpio Jupiter can represent hidden or secret beliefs and/or (occult) wisdom. Scorpio Jupiter understands the magical power of belief. S/he really gets the new adage: "I will see it when I believe it."

Pisces: Pisces Jupiter *just knows* the answer to many things. The only thing that can hinder this is lack of trust in your own intelligence. This is the placement of high spiritual advancement:

Expanding Consciousness: Jupiter

Outlining Creativity: Saturn

Life on Earth is dualistic and may be symbolized by respiration or tidal motion. In the process of life, we alternate between pushing-our-limits and contracting energy into form. That duality is represented by Expansion/Jupiter and Contraction/Saturn. Jupiter every pushes Saturn outward, while Saturn provides safe limits for growth. Their periodic conjunctions show us when to *take the next step upward or outward.*

As we evolve, the esoteric purpose of Saturn emerges. Saturn represents our capacity to separate the specific from the general, to focus on a portion of the whole. It is the means by which we see what we choose to see, causing it to emerge from the background of visible possibilities. Likewise, it allows us to hear what we are listening to, sorting it out from the general mass of sound. Saturn performs similar functions for all the physical senses, so that we can focus on what is important to us.

It is interesting to notice that, in the past, Saturn has been regarded as a limit or a roadblock, something we could not get past. But the simple truth is that Saturn is always a self-generated limit, designed for our protection from that which we are not ready to focus our attention upon. Notice that, in the solar system, Jupiter's expansion is always behind Saturn's limits. This is because those limits are meant to expand as we mature. At the beginning of life, our spacial limit may be a crib, then a room, the house, the yard, the neighborhood, and so on. By the end of life, our limits may be the world, while at the end of many lifetimes, they may be the galaxy, the universe, and/or eternity. By sign, Saturn ever sets the kind of limits we use for these purposes. As our skeleton and skin hold our body together, so Saturn holds our lives together.

A focus is extended to become a definition or *word*. When we name a thing, we outline it, excluding the background. Naming actions or events is the same. In a sense the difference between god-hood and human-hood is vested here. Divine awareness is the awareness of totality. It is impersonal. Human awareness is specifically focused and personal. Ultimately, we are the personalized expression of divinity, focused into specific experience, the operative arm of Spirit. A most important part of self-realization is the recognition that, as Spirit is creative, so its physical expression (I/we) is/are also creative. According to Genesis, "In the beginning God spoke . . . and it was so." This sets the principle of the creative word. It is the basis of the creative consciousness, which focuses on a word/idea, and in so doing, brings it into manifest expression.

Saturn's role in the creative process is then to name and define reality. Historically, reality has been thought to be fixed. As we evolve, we learn to envision or verbalize an outline of what we wish to create. That outline becomes a type of void or vacuum. Since the Universe abhors a vacuum, it will fill that outline. The specific infilling is ruled by Venus and the principle of like attracts like. An outline of a car will be filled in with car *substance*.

Saturn is also law or rules. Most of the so-called *moral laws* are clearly man-made, and for a variety of reasons, not all of them related to the *life and greater life* which is the divine intent for humanity. However, there are some basic laws of function; like the *laws of science*, they are meant to teach us how things work. Certain of these laws apply to the use of the creative consciousness. We have mentioned two above. We need also to note the underlying causes of seeming creative failures.

When we are working with the Divine/Universal substance/energy, we must follow Saturn's rules if we are to achieve the desired results. The most basic of these is that, at this level, all things work together for good.

Humans—especially those born before the 1970s—were conditioned by the adults who were in charge of their physical childhood. To a large degree, they shaped our basic ideas and values. That taught us what we *should want, should have, should do, etc.*, and how to go about getting it. What they taught us was based on their experience and their location in time and space. A great deal of what we learned was obsolete by the time we came of age. Some of it was very much against our own self-interest. To the degree that we absorbed it as truth—and for many that was a large degree—we began our ventures into use of the creative consciousness by attempting to create things that were of no use, or of no value, to the lives we were reaching for.

Consequently, creation of the amount of money we needed to buy a car might come with a bill of equal or even greater size. We got the money, but not the car. Others clearly defined the car—a blue corvette with racing stripes—got that, but it did not run, or it required endless repairs. From this we may learn to phrase our creative focus differently. If we want transportation, we ask for the right transportation, the best transportation, the transportation that will meet all our needs. Transportation will then be provided, sometimes in surprising ways, but always in ways that serve us well.

The creative consciousness is designed to provide our true needs, desires, and even hopes and wishes. The key is to use Saturn to correctly outline our requests, taking into account the fact that many of us are not completely in touch with our own best interest. Still, we can trust that our creative consciousness—by any name (subconscious, super-consciousness, God/dess, angels)—does know what to create in service of our own best interests. If we trust that all we need to do is to sketch the outlines of our creative focus, leaving the details to the invisible power/intelligence that moves through us all.

In conclusion, we affirm that Saturn is the principle of limiting outlines. However, we deny its intent to limit our lives, our growth, our awareness. It is, instead, a protective limit designed to keep us from taking risks beyond our current maturity level.

Let us each realize that every boundary is intended to protect temporarily, then to expand, to grow, to move as we mature. Saturnian limits are no more solid and rigid than the horizon. Walk toward them and they will maintain a certain distance ahead of you. *They are your protection, not your prison.*

Saturn in the Elements and Signs

Saturn in Fire

Saturn in fire ultimately refers to *spiritual limits*. It requires us to focus on spirit and its potential and to realize that our physical being is simply a form that spirit takes, not a prison in which it is trapped.

Aries: Although it can manifest as survival fears, Aries Saturn is limited only by our level of self-awareness. Often natives accept far too much from others, only drawing the line at their skin. Many have a tendency to be *daredevils* when young, feeling some need to prove their indestructibility.

Leo: Saturn in Leo is intended to be no more, and no differently limited than the Sun. Leo Saturn is really the reach of personal radiation, otherwise understood as influence or reputation. Personal limits would then be at the outer edge of the aura, resembling the Sun's corona. However, at present Leo Saturn often still manifests as *inherited limits*. These refer to a general belief that I cannot do something because *our family* does not, cannot, or will not do it, or because I do not have (have not inherited) the talent.

Sagittarius: Saturn in Sagittarius understands limits and is intended to be *traveling limits*. This placement makes the horizon our only real limit—and it moves as we move toward it. However, it frequently starts out as *limits of belief*. Literally it means that our limits are where we believe them to be.

Saturn in Earth

Saturn in earth refers to (perceived) physical limits. Many natives use their body condition to limit progress to a pace which feels safe. Others may confine themselves to a particular locality, explaining this to themselves in various ways.

Taurus: Taurus Saturn is most often expressed as *financial limits*. This is usually based on low self-worth. If you do not believe that you are worth much, the economy will confirm your belief, and your resources will be limited.

Virgo: Virgo Saturn is most often expressed as *limits of duty*, of conscience, of guilt. It can feel like limited usefulness, but this is, *invariably*, a conditioned response. The great lesson of your life is that, although you may wish to serve, *you are not a servant*. You can serve as a boss or a professional.

An alternate expression of Virgo Saturn is *limits of health*. When conditioned (religious) *duty* collides with innate (spiritual) intent, ill health provides a socially acceptable means of avoiding the choice.

Capricorn: Capricorn Saturn is limited only by the current definition of humanity. This placement shows the intention to push the very limits of what most believe is possible to humans. If you have limited success in life, it can only be because you need to expand your beliefs about human possibility. Your commitment is to expand the current definition of the word human, to include more of the divine potential in us all.

Saturn in Air

Saturn in air is a spacial limit and can make you feel that you have no room to expand. Like so many Saturn effects, this one is a misperception, based on conditioned beliefs. The more air you use, the more you will have. The more space you make/claim (in your relationships), the more you will have.

Gemini: Gemini limits are words. This Saturn claims space by simply naming it and more space by renaming it. Natives *must* listen to themselves, noticing how often they speak limiting words once spoken to them. The real key to growth is an expanding vocabulary and/or learning to choose positive words in place of negatives. This is especially important in your creative activities. The subconscious does not recognize negatives. Consequently, when you tell it, "I do not want _____," it promptly produces the very thing you did not want.

Libra: Libra's limits are often relationships, but only when those relationships are unbalanced, unequal. Associate with equals, or reach upward, and these limits will disappear. The real issue here is whether you maintain a balance between your humanity and your divinity, between the intake and outflow of information. At its best, Libra is a conversation, *not an oration*. This is what is meant by the biblical instruction for the assembling of like-minded individuals. When these share, all increase awareness.

This is equally true of an appropriate marital union. If both partners increase awareness, it is a success. If not, it becomes a limit on at least one partner.

Aquarius: Aquarius limits are *out of sight*—literally they are galactic in size. They are the signature of one born *more than man*—according to the current definition. This is the mark of the Adept or the High Priest/tess.

These limits are adaptable and can be changed at will. Because they are the limits of change, if you resist change, you limit yourself. If you stay open, if you learn to adapt, your limits expand. Literally, you are only limited by your openness to greater possibilities. Staying open brings the inspiration that can take you to universal and eternal information and the potential to re-create your world.

Saturn in Water

Water Saturn limits are fluid, changing according to our perception of needs. Consequently, they are intended to mature with us. How you handle your emotions is a product of how well you handle your needs. The more dependant you are on others, the more limited you will be. The more independent you are, the less limited you will be.

Feelings are the *mind of the body*. They tell us what we need for physical comfort and well-being. Emotions are the outward motions of reaching for those needs, the action we take to support and supply our lives. Because the Moon represents our initial needs, it is important to work with it. Its sign will tell us what we came into this life needing. However, as time passes, we learn to fulfill many of those needs and our need-system is designed to mature accordingly. Problems arise when we do not leave infantile needs behind as we move into adulthood. Consequently the Exercise given may be needed to help you reach clarity about your real, current, needs.

Cancer: Cancer Saturn usually has limits conditioned by its birth. Your initial limits may actually belong to mother or family. The neediness you felt in your birth family has been absorbed as your own, but it does not really belong to you. This can form a habit of absorbing the needs of anyone physically close to you. Look to your Sun's sign to determine what you really need. You may also need to do some boundary work.

Scorpio: Scorpio Saturn is about the *limits of power*, secret limits, and/or the limiting power of secrets. Natives may have secret limits that control their use of personal power, making them afraid of misusing their personal power. Traditionally, large segments of the population have feared power, because it is subject to misuse. If this Saturn regards control—especially lack of control—as a limiting factor, Scorpio Saturn may limit your control of your own life.

Much depends on your understanding of Pluto/Scorpio power. This kind of power is *simply the ability to do*, and especially the ability to create/control your own life as you choose. It was never intended to be used for the control or abuse of other people by emotional means. (That means fear, anger or seduction.)

Scorpio is about the power available in Union. In the sexual context, it is the very power that creates life. In the spiritual context, as a union with Deity, it becomes the power to transform reality. This placement has the potential to completely transform your life. First use Saturn to outline your life as you wish it to be. Then imagine Pluto as a huge magnet which attracts the substance to fill that outline. This will work, to the degree that you believe it will.

Pisces: Pisces Saturn is unconscious or *forgotten* boundaries because this placement shows one who is Master of Boundaries. In other words, these people have mastered the entire principle during previous incarnations and have no boundaries of their own. Because they do not, they easily absorb certain boundaries from others (parents, spouses), but only where they are initially conditioned to have boundaries. Consequently, in other areas they seem to walk right through what observers consider boundaries. To the watcher, they often do the improbable, sometimes the *impossible*.

Still, natives may spend half their lives or more, trying to overcome absorbed limits. The only real cure is to forget those limits, to erase them from consciousness, and to trust their own *gut instincts* about what is right, wrong, possible or impossible for them to do. This will require the realization that only those who are spiritually mature can have such a placement. They, quite literally, *cannot do the wrong thing*, for their true *limits* are absorbed from their Deity.

The great gift of this placement is that there really is no limit to what these can do/be/become, to what they can change/create/transform. They are the adult offspring of their God/dess with management positions in the *family business* and authorized to speak for their Deity.

The Identity Structure: Uranus

Mars, Chiron, Eris, Jupiter, and Saturn show our interaction with others, with society, with localized time and space. They symbolize our ordinary, everyday, purely-human function. Beginning with Uranus, we move beyond Earth, to the greater realities of outer space and future time. The final three planets call us to remember our divine genetics, to develop our intuitive and creative side, to recognize that the Child of God must grow into its adult godhood, to become more than *merely human*.

Humans, individually and collectively, reincarnate repeatedly as a means of growing into our spiritual genetics. Science has told us that we have large unused areas in both our DNA and our brain. We believe that the three outer planets represent our potential to expand into formerly unused areas of being and consciousness. The three outer planets are our symbolic vehicles for this expansion.

Our reincarnational journey is intended to take us *beyond Earth*, into Universal and then Cosmic citizenship. This is our heritage as (literal) offspring of our God/dess. We believe that human evolution is simply a matter of self-discovery, of learning to use more of our innate potential.

Below the plane of Jupiter and Saturn, and directly beneath Mars, we place Uranus, the final Identity marker: the Universal/Eternal Identity.

Uranus is the final planet in the human identity structure. Uranus may be called Higher Self or Son/daughter of the Universe. S/he represents impersonal beingness, that part of us which is connected and/or committed to serving all-human purposes. When we move into our Uranian Identity, we begin to claim our divine genetics, our galactic and cosmic citizenship.

Whether latent or active, somewhere within each of us is a hope or wish to leave a mark on history, to do something that will benefit humanity. For many generations, this has largely been denied and ignored by our caretakers. We were urged to be logical, practical, to remain within the parameters of the current definition of humanity, as bounded by Saturn and Capricorn.

This left little room for children to develop the intuitive skills which connect us to the unseen realms. Outer space was out of sight and best left alone. We were taught that God was in charge and needed no help from us. Consequently, many stopped seeing what the adults could not see, stopped hearing what they could not hear. To do otherwise risked exorcism or, more recently, psychiatric treatment, often involving drugs.

Our Universal Identity was ignored, suppressed, denied. And because it was, it took *an act of God* to break it out of conditioned chains. For individuals, that event was often signaled by a transit of Uranus. When Saturn's limits become too tight, too rigid, when we cannot or will not expand them, it is Uranus' task to break them.

As the planet of sudden change, of surprises, coincidences, and accidents Uranus has sometimes been regarded as a rogue, or some outside force that disrupts our plans. With the advent of

Chaos theory, we catch a glimpse of the *higher rationale* of Uranus. The only thing that makes Uranian events seem sudden is following Saturn's dictates and keeping our focus on practical things which fall within the realm of those planets inside Saturn's orbit. Many still teach that anything beyond Saturn is dark, but the news is spreading. We—each and all of us—carry the light, and it is our eventual task to become the light-bearers of the galaxy and cosmos. Uranus stands for the light-bearer in each of us. Some call this our light-body.

Uranus represents that part of our beingness that is *different from the norm*. Uranian rhythms are *not of this earth*, or *not of this time*. They represent a much larger cyclic pattern than recognized by traditionalists. The transits of Uranus seem sudden or unexpected because it has a larger orbit and its effects fall outside the ordinary routines of life. When orbiting Uranus touches a natal planet, our higher purpose is trying to break us out of our Earthbound limits. It is calling to that part of our identity which recognizes our universal citizenship. Hence the Uranus-Uranus opposition becomes a turning point in many lives, as we reach beyond Saturn's *limits of reason* to Uranus' unlimited possibilities.

Some call Uranus self-centered. In reality it is higher-self-centered. Uranus calls us to leave behind much of what we have learned as duty, lest we use up the gifts given us for the world, in serving the dependencies of a few *spiritually lazy* individuals. When Uranus calls, it is time to stop listening to individual voices and start listening to the Universal call, or the Voice of our God/dess. That higher call will return us to the purpose for which we incarnated.

To be fully identified with Uranus is to live *between the worlds*. It is the mark of the priest/ess who stands between heaven and earth. S/he lifts the prayers of the people, and speaks for the God/dess. The great purpose of Uranians everywhere is to carry the light, to be the light. This is the Uranian message:

You came from the Stars, Seeds containing sparks
You came to grow, to expand the light
Your mission is, one day
To relight the stars from which you came.

Uranus in the Elements and Signs

Uranus in Fire

Uranus in fire is lit up, aflame, like a comet streaking across the night. In a personal horoscope it indicates a higher mind with its citizenship in something larger than ordinary Earth parameters. It is citizen of the Future, of the Galaxy, of the Universe. This is the placement for transcendent change, and natives become a catalyst for change—not merely in the individuals around them, but also in general attitudes. Their changes demonstrate new possibilities to all those whose lives they touch.

Aries: Uranus in Aries is the placement of the *Seed Being*. S/he plants the seeds of the future. S/he impulses expansion of consciousness in the general population. The ultimate *misfit*, these are born to lead—not in space, but in time. They are pioneers in consciousness. Sometimes they even transcend death, reviving time after time, to prove that we are all immortal.

Leo: Uranus in Leo is the placement of the *Light Bearer*. Intended to be *the light of the world*, these live out the possibilities inherent in changing roles. They can almost *be all things to all people*. Let no one criticize their sometimes chameleon-like coloration. They shine their light at whatever frequency is needed at the time.

Sagittarius: Uranus in Sagittarius is a prophet, a *Messenger from the Future*. They are the trailblazers, the map-makers for the next age. They are true Aquarians who have stepped back in time to help us across the hindering boundaries in existing belief systems. Like the disciples who ushered in the Age of Pisces, these carry the *good news* that we are more and better than we knew.

Uranus in Earth

Uranus in earth demonstrates the possibilities in changing form, function, and/or goals. These natives are focused on the pragmatic. They teach us how to apply *higher knowledge* to the practicalities of daily living. Ultimately, theirs is the task of transcending old forms through the recognition that a body is simply a visible, tangible form that spirit takes. Changes come through recognition of the spiritual potential within any physical form.

Taurus: Taurus Uranus is a *Shape Changer*. Initially, they change the shape of their own lives, often from the traditional to the non-traditional. Many do not become fully realized until their early forties, when they do an about-face, give up trying to find their *place* within society, and move to a place in front of it, assuming their leadership in building the future. Their lives are shaped by the *impersonal mission* for which they were born, the *impersonal role* for which they incarnated.

Virgo: Virgo Uranus is the *Function Changer*, demonstrating new ways to use their lives. They ultimately dedicate their bent for service to a higher purpose. This one may change jobs at mid-life—or even as late as their early fifties. They may regain lost health, often as a result of changing their entire mode of action. This is the placement of the *Servant of the Most High*.

Capricorn: Capricorn Uranus is the *Definition Changer*—one committed to changing and expanding the current definition of humanity. It is about changing the old *limits of possibility to unlimited possibilities*—and the maturation of humanity into a full co-creative partnership with Deity. These are the managers of society who help to create new parameters and rules for society.

Uranus in Air

Uranus in air is a *Relationship Changer*. It is one inspired in ways that lift relationships to a higher level, making them impersonal. Impersonal relationships are spiritual relationships based upon our Divine DNA. They function at a higher, more abstract level, because they are more about humanity than about individual humans. This is the place where lower and higher mind meet and human consciousness meets God consciousness. It is the realization that being Children of Deity means growing up to be like the Divine Parent.

Gemini: Gemini is the sign of the sibling, so Gemini Uranus points to the Uranian Brotherhood. These natives are *Elder Brothers*, on Earth at this time to aid in the raising of consciousness in their younger siblings, peers, and neighbors. They have stepped back in time and have the ability almost to live in two worlds simultaneously—moving between them.

Libra: Libra is the sign of partnership. Libra Uranus points to a union with the Divine. It is the *inner marriage* spoken of in esoteric writings. This is the placement of the *New Age Nun/Monk*, who is *married to Deity*. These have grown up to become partners in the Divine Business of parenting humanity as it grows into its potential.

Aquarius: Aquarius Uranus is *Friend of God and Man*, the true adept, the master magician with the ability to change the world. Sometimes assuming the role of the rebel, other times authoring *declarations of independence*, they are the instigators of sweeping changes in this world.

This placement always indicates a new cycle of change comparable to the industrial revolution or the information age. During the seven-year period of this transit, the very course of human life changes as it makes the next step in human evolution. Certain individuals, born within this period, will become major players in that process.

Uranus in Water

Uranus in water is fluid, takes the shape of the container, and finds its own level. This Uranus is a *Level Changer*. Change flows naturally from cycle to cycle. As one circle ends, the next is lifted into a spiral. Water Uranus may bring a change in the course of the *river of life*. This placement points to the fact that the more flexible we are, the more conscious we become. The more conscious we are, the more knowledge will flow through us.

Cancer: Cancer Uranus is emerging from the previous cycle, being reborn at a higher level. This placement shows *Spiritual Growth*. Here Cancer is more *rebirth* than birth. One phase of development ends and a new phase begins, bringing a new type/cycle of growth in awareness. Its gift is empathy.

Scorpio: Scorpio Uranus is empowered. This is the placement of *Spiritual Investment*, of being anointed and/or ordained to a higher priesthood. This can be the true magician and/or the trance channel. They are invested with power and authorized to use it to create change in the world. Sometimes they are honored. Sometimes they are cursed. Always they are beloved of God, for they take on tasks that few others would accept.

Pisces: Pisces Uranus is *Master of Change*. They may be individuals who repeatedly incarnate at the turning points in human evolution and/or the cusp periods at the changing of the ages. These are not here to do anything specific. They are simply the human catalysts who create change by their very presence. Most are not religious. All are spiritual. Like the Masters of old, they walk through life, leaving change in their wake.

Higher Consciousness: Neptune

Chiron, Eris, Jupiter and Saturn show our interaction with others, with society, with localized time and space. They symbolize our ordinary, everyday, purely human function. Having mastered that, we move into Higher Self.

Our final division is composed of Uranus/Identity, Neptune/ Higher Consciousness, and Pluto/Higher Creativity. Together, they provide our connections to the galaxy and cosmos. The final triad is our link to All-That-Is.

It is our thesis that humans, individually and collectively, reincarnate repeatedly as a means of growing into awareness of our spiritual genetics. Science has told us that we have large unused areas in both our DNA and our brain. We believe that the three outer planets represent our potential to expand into formerly unused areas of being and consciousness. This is our heritage as (literal) offspring of our God/dess. We believe that human evolution is simply a matter of self-discovery, of learning to use those increasing areas of our potential and that the discovery of

Chiron signaled the arrival of the necessary *critical mass* needed to lift humanity up sufficiently to enter the next age.

Neptune is the final planet in the human consciousness structure. It represents all our forgotten knowledge—knowledge that exists outside our usual focus of attention. In this area, we find buried records from our earliest years, including those from the pre-verbal period along with memories repressed for various reasons. These files include our species data and whatever else is under the umbrella of the autonomic nervous system. They also include past lives and the knowledge acquired from them, much of which manifests as talents and abilities in this life time. Ultimately, Neptune represents our potential for mastery of (the totality of) consciousness. It promises eventual access to all that is in our personal memory files, all that is in human memory, and, in time, all the files of the Universe. Neptune's sign tells us something about our personal quest for and approaches to mastery. Behind Neptune stands the timeless, space-less, background field of awareness and intelligence generally called Universal Consciousness, or Akashic Record. Potentially, it extends even farther to include what might be called the *mind of God/dess*.

In practice, Neptune represents our capacity to become aware of all that resides outside our ordinary perceptual field. We gradually learn techniques that allow us to use Neptunian realms. These include various divinitory techniques, hypnosis, and meditation. Imagine that beyond the World Wide Web is an Eternal Universal Web. Our mind cannot really grasp such a field of awareness. It is too large. Reaching for it causes our mental focus to blur. In time, we develop greater and easier access to this *cosmic internet*.

This is the principle behind Neptune transits. Under them we are stretching the reach of our awareness, and it takes a bit of practice before we can focus into the new range clearly. At this point, we are required to trust the process, assuming that our *vision* will clear. Experience teaches us that it always does.

Neptune has been compared to smoke or fog, but today it may be more like the horizon. We can see it but never entirely grasp it because when we move toward it, it moves ahead of us. In principle it represents all that lies beyond the scope of ordinary awareness, beyond the scope of the physical senses. It is what we cannot see, hear, touch, or know *in the ordinary way*, because it is beyond the reach of our physical senses—thus includes what is called extra-sensory-perception.

Our perceptions are confined by the quality or development of our senses and we speak of *the invisible or the inaudible*. But the truth is that such areas are simply beyond the range of our physical eyes and ears. More likely, they are only beyond what we have learned that we can or should see and/or hear. This clearly varies. Some people can see ghosts or auras, while many cannot. Some can hear the thoughts of others: incarnate, discarnate, or both. Others cannot.

Each of our senses, most obviously sight and hearing, functions within a specific range comparable to the bands of visible light and audible sound. As we evolve over lifetimes, our senses are intended to expand this range. They do not always expand at the same rate, and the various psychics/intuitives demonstrate this. A clairvoyant may not be clairaudient, or vice versa. Most people begin by developing their emotional sensitivity in the form of empathy. This is followed by the gradual development of the ability to acquire information through the inner eyes and/or ears.

So long as we use *only* the physical senses, Neptune can produce little beyond dreams. In time we can learn to interpret dreams, and from there move into the intuitive range of the senses. Then, as we evolve, Neptune's realm expands into Universal Mind. Like modern computers, we learn to access and use a great deal that lies beyond our physical senses, even what may lie beyond our physical beingness. Neptune is the totality and human evolution is the process of learning to focus attention at greater and greater ranges within and beyond the totality of time and space.

The next step in human evolution has been heralded by the discovery of Chiron, which symbolizes a long-dormant modem, newly awakened in humanity. Since the early 1930s, and the discovery of Pluto, the use of the Chiron function has been potential for us all. However, that was not general knowledge. In many the function was suppressed to one extent or another. Then, generation by generation, more individuals dared to explore previously unknown ranges of human consciousness. At a certain point this group grew large enough to make an impression on the general consciousness. Critical mass, symbolized by Chiron, marked the beginning stages of the rising baseline for the general consciousness. From this point, all newborns arrived on Earth with the potential to develop a whole new range of awareness.

Today's children are able to see, hear, and sense more than any generation in history. Some older adults have activated Chiron, retrieving gifts put away in childhood. The people born in recent decades came in with Chiron already fully activated at birth. To some they seem a new species. To the wise they represent the awakening of humanity to more of its innate potential.

The quickening of the Chiron function, individually and generally, is extending our senses in the same way that a modem extends the range and usefulness of our personal computers. It makes the Neptune function far more accessible than it was before the 1970s. Human consciousness is expanding into fields of awareness not even imagined a few decades ago.

Finally, Neptune is visionary. A vision is the first step in creating anything. An idea is a symbol for a vision. These are the components that make visualizations and affirmations work. As we become more adept, we begin to use increasing areas of the human brain. The movement that takes us deeper into Neptune's realm is the journey we undertake as we approach the next age. Neptune's message is this:

Intuition is the remembrance of past and future learning.
It exists in the timeless reality.
All that you know, you have learned In this lifetime or another.
Intuition is logic, functioning at the speed of light.
Trust it. Trust its visions.
Imagine remembering how to create what you want.
Daydream your way to Heaven on Earth.

Neptune in the Elements and Signs

Neptune in Fire

Neptune in fire is Spiritual Mastery, and based on humanity's quest to know its origins, to know its Deity. Its approach is direct, based on an innate sense that we are related to a Higher Power and that we have the capacity to develop higher abilities because of it.

Aries: Aries Neptune represents inception, the impulse toward a new level of development. It is the *breath of life* that transforms the higher animal into a lesser god. The Aries Neptune natives of the future, will pioneer new developments in human consciousness. They are the true Seed Beings who will be catalysts for a major expansion in the general consciousness during the next age.

It will be the late 2070s before the next generation of Leo Neptune natives is born. Conscious of their Divine heritage, this group will dissolve traditionally inherited roles of incarnate life, creating models for an Aquarian Society. These are the active masters of life, no longer identifying as created beings, but as pro-created by Deity. They have claimed their spiritual heritage, and new areas of their DNA have awakened. They know that they are Divine Sons/Daughters, by *blood*, neither adopted children nor indentured servants of their God/dess.

Sagittarius: Sagittarius Neptune is a Divine Messenger and/or teacher to older generations. Today's bright future shines through the current generation of children born with Neptune in Sagittarius. Their message is that belief is creative, that when we believe in magic and miracles, we will see them. They are here to teach their elders the true nature of spirituality, to go beyond religion to the reality of our innate spirituality.

Neptune in Earth

Neptune in earth represents Grounded Spiritual Mastery. These are the practical masters of life who live out mundane applications of faith. They are the living proof that there is a spiritual purpose to every facet of human life, and that to become fully invested spiritual beings requires time spent applying spiritual principles to physical living.

Taurus: Taurus Neptune represents the embodiment of spirit. Its particular task is to prove the value of the incarnate form as a phase of spiritual development. In practical terms, these natives may fund spiritual projects or become the temple-builders of the future.

Virgo: Virgo Neptune represents the uses and mastery of Spiritual Techniques. When Neptune crossed Virgo, during the 1930s and 1940s, humans began to be born with a fully developed physical structure in which consciousness could be raised to the level demonstrated by Jesus ben Joseph some two thousand years ago. They started the seeding process that led to critical mass in the late 1970s.

Many of the oldest spiritual leaders of today were born during the last Neptune passage through Virgo. Resistance from their elders caused many/most of them to forget their special abilities. Only a few retrieved those gifts in later years. Those few are to be honored for their courage and persistence, and for setting the first examples of how to use the spiritual gifts and the greater awareness that was becoming increasingly conscious in each new Neptune generation.

Capricorn: Capricorn Neptune is a fully matured Practical Master. These are living proof of what began in the 1930s and 1940s. In them this facility has become automatic. They demonstrate an automatic creativity that proves the power of belief, as never before. Those who grew up relatively free of conditioning are the hope of our future. Others, coerced to condemn these new abilities, prove to the world that they are as crazy or evil as they have been taught to believe that they are.

Neptune in Air

Neptune in air is intended to mean Mastery of Space, Time and Thought. It is the point where the intuitive-creative right brain achieves dominance over the left-brain. It points to the potential to evolve the senses to include much wider perceptual ranges. Natives may begin to see, hear, or otherwise sense much that is beyond the generally accepted parameters of perception.

Gemini: Gemini Neptune is the telepath. This placement shows the ability to hear the thoughts of others. Initially, it may seem to be confined to those in parallel relationships (like siblings and peers), but with practice can be developed further. A great gift of this placement is that it has an *on-off* switch, unlike other types of intuitive gifts.

The evolutionary process has begun in the general population with the appearance of the Crystal Children, beginning in the late 1990s. By the time humanity evolves to the period of the next Neptune in Gemini generation, spoken language may disappear.

Libra: Libra Neptune is the medium. Natives are able to share consciousness with other beings, and to channel the thoughts of others, incarnate and/or discarnate. Generally, this talent is confined to the trance state, when the wisdom of discarnate beings is dispensed through borrowed incarnate forms. For this to be possible, there must be equality between the two beings. To channel accurately, the host being must have some knowledge of the subject to be channeled. The partnership between them, allows wider applications from basic principles. This ability will improve and applications will widen by the next passage of Neptune through Libra.

Aquarius: Aquarius Neptune is God Consciousness—the next step beyond the Christ Consciousness which was the gift of the Age of Pisces. Literally, these arrive with awareness expanded to the level that will be the baseline for humanity in the Age of Aquarius. It is the consciousness type which has been called genius during the current age, and refers to the capacity to focus into various realities at will, combining their resources. Sometimes called conscious channeling this is a highly practical skill of the type that produces both art and invention.

Many of the current generation born with Neptune in Aquarius are being misdiagnosed in a variety of ways, because they are so obviously different from earlier generations. They totally violate many of the criteria established by the medical profession. Many are initially thought to be deaf or autistic because speech development is retarded. And yet, alert parents may notice that these children respond very well to parental thought.

Neptune in Water

Neptune in Water is intended to mean Master of Flow and/or Master of Feelings and Emotions. Traditionally, the water element as a metaphor has been confined to the emotional flow of feelings through which physical needs are expressed. In people born before the Indigo generations, this was often problematical because the feeling structure was usually absorbed from the mother and/or primary caretaker. This left natives responding to needs that belonged to the person to whom they initially bonded. When that happened a transformation process was required before natives could be clear about their true needs. Until the need-system was cleared, the possibility of getting and keeping values, desires, and needs was often hobbled.

The great blessing (and curse) for recent generations is that they are born with their need systems already fully formed and intact. When parents were able to recognize this, it was a great blessing and children progressed rapidly. When parents insisted on forcing their ideas and values upon these children, explosions of varying magnitude happened. Rage at what felt like personal violation powered various outbreaks of violence among the Indigo generations.

The Indigos were followed by the Crystal Children, many of whom have Indigo parents. While the Indigos were/are systems-busters, here to shake things up and create dramatic change, Crystals are peacemakers and their way is passive resistance. When elders try to change them, these children simply *shut them out of consciousness* and ignore them. This capacity may be responsible for much misdiagnosed autism.

Cancer: The ultimate meaning of Cancer is emergence—from the dark/unknown, from the womb, from the soil. Cancer Neptune is, then, Emerging Mastery. It refers to the early realization that it is possible to understand how consciousness works and to master the process of increasing awareness. A very few recognized this during the last passage of Neptune through Cancer, producing some great thinkers and psychics. For the most part, we must look to the future, when the growth-factor of emergence will again become highly visible. Nothing grows so rapidly as a newborn, so we can expect some very rapid maturation during the next transit of Neptune through Cancer.

Scorpio: Scorpio Neptune is the Mental Magician, able to perform extraordinary feats with mind- power. This placement merges the inherently Plutonian creative consciousness with the higher aspects of intelligence. Natives have the gift of intensifying mental energy to the point of physical manifestation. The recognition of this potential began with the last passage of Neptune through Scorpio. Only a few natives had need-systems sufficiently clear to use these new powers easily and productively. Still, scattered among the population we find those who are able *magically* to produce money, jobs, and possessions. They are the prototypes for human acceptance of our divinely inherited mantle of power.

Pisces: Neptune in Pisces is at its peak. Literally translated, it means Master of Life. It is the awareness that each of us is, in some way, an *anointed one*, a christed being. It is the innate knowledge that as a *child of God*, we are destined to grow up to be like the Divine Parent.

In practice it would mean one who could use the human form of all the spiritual gifts. As God/dess is omniscient, we are clairvoyant/clairaudient/clairsentient. As it is omnipresent, we can do astral travel, perhaps teleportation. As it is omnipotent, we have developed our magical abilities. Beginning in 2012, a new generation of Pisces Neptune natives began to be born. Let us hope that the world is better prepared for them.

This may well be the *second coming of Christ(hood)*. They will model the fulfillment of the Piscean Age. They will be the final AMEN before the beginning of the next cycle of human evolution. Humanity is growing up!

Higher Creativity: Pluto

Chiron, Eris, Jupiter, and Saturn show our interaction with others, with society, and with localized time and space. They symbolize our ordinary, everyday, purely human function. Beginning with Uranus, we move beyond Earth to the greater realities of outer space and future time. The final three planets call us to remember our divine genetics, to develop our intuitive and creative side, to recognize that the Child of God must grow into its adult godhood, to become more than *merely human*.

It is our thesis that humans, individually and collectively, reincarnate repeatedly as a means of growing into our spiritual genetics. Science has told us that we have large unused areas in both our DNA and our brain. We believe that the three outer planets represent our potential to expand into formerly unused areas of being and consciousness.

Our reincarnational journey is intended to take us *beyond Earth*, into Universal and then Cosmic citizenship. This is our heritage as (literal) offspring of our God/dess. Human evolution is simply a matter of self-discovery, of learning to use those increasing areas of our potential.

The final division is composed of Uranus/Identity, Neptune/Consciousness and Pluto/Creativity. Together, they provide our connections to the galaxy and cosmos. The final triad is our link to All-That-Is.

Pluto is the final planet in the human creativity structure. It represents personal power, the ability to do. It represents the power to know, to know who, what, and why we are. It represents creative power, the power to create and recreate our lives.

It is not about the use of coercion or force. It is not about manipulating others. It is not about control, beyond rational self-control. It is not about blackmail, emotional or otherwise.

Pluto's personal power is simply about recognizing our ability to change, transform, create, revise, and shape our own lives by investing our attention in that which is of real personal value to us. Traditionally, it has been an essentially adult asset, for it was assumed that all power belonged in the hands of adults. Today we have begun to recognize the potency of the clear, inner-child state. In that state of consciousness which is innocent of flaws—as every newborn is—lies the truest and safest power of all, the ultimate and absolute power of love.

In its essence this refers to the recognition of the value in all of life. The greatest word-power of all is the power inherent in naming a thing "good." And the greatest frustration of all, lies in trying to create something for yourself, when you have named that thing "bad/evil." Witness the great struggle to develop a prosperity consciousness. Money is not the root of evil. It is merely the symbol for earned reserves of energy—energy which can be spent in the creation of greater good. The point is not to obsess about or hoard money for its own sake, but to honor it by investing it for the greater good.

Still new, in human consciousness, we are only beginning to discover the human potential for magical creation, the ability to create using attention as focused through a word or idea.

In every natal chart, Pluto represents personal power. We have been learning about personal power since the discovery of Pluto in 1930. For the most part, the first several Pluto generations simply confronted their lack of power, noticing where it went. The Cancer generation confronted the power that mother/family has over us. The Leo generation confronted hereditary roles. The Virgo generation confronted issues of guilt and duty. The Libra generation confronted the power of Society, especially as it was vested in conventional notions of marriage. The Scorpio generation confronted sin, and especially issues of sexual sin. In Sagittarius, Pluto confronted us with the power of our beliefs. Currently in Capricorn, Pluto confronts us with the limits in our current definition of the word *human*.

Before we can use Pluto in any personal way, we must first confront our lack of power. The simple meaning of Pluto is really, "I can _____." For the earlier Pluto generations, this was very limited. We often found ourselves saying, "I cannot _____ because it would offend my parents, because our family does not do such things, because it is not nice, because I am married."

Gradually a shift began. People started to experiment with the creative consciousness in the form of affirmation, visualization, and ritual. That triggered a confrontation with our beliefs. We discovered that, no matter how much we want a thing, if we believe it is wrong to have, we cannot create it. We cannot move fully into our Higher Self or Light Body, until we face and heal our wounded souls. This is the transforming power of Pluto. He requires that we let go much of our conditioning, emptying our hands of the past, before we can claim Pluto's power to create our future. We must let go our negative self-judgments, realizing that we are the perfect offspring of a perfect Deity. Only then will our potential for creative power become fully available.

Initially, Pluto represents rebirth, or more accurately, metamorphosis. As any Pluto transit approaches, we find ourselves tied up in a cocoon of old habits and/or beliefs. For a time our lives seem completely stalled, even regressing. Think of this as the larvae stage. We enter the transforming metamorphosis in the old larvae shape, but will emerge in the shape, the glory, of a butterfly—no longer earthbound, our consciousness rises on wings of light.

The first task in our search for personal power must be that of Self-Awareness. We must become aware of ourselves as more than created beings. We are pro-creations of Original Being. We are offspring, not robots! As offspring, we inherit the potential to be-all, see-all, know all. More than that, we inherit the ability to create and re-create our own reality. It is all in our divine genetics.

Science speaks of the double-helix genetic structure. We like to think that it is composed of one physical strand and one spiritual strand. Today humanity is beginning to achieve awareness of new possibilities—possibilities that were always inherent in the human structure.

As we complete our astrological tree of life, we find science and spirit coming together. Even as we inherit certain physical abilities from our Earthly parents, so also, we inherit certain spiritual abilities from our Divine parent. The final stage of doing that (at least for the closing Age of Pisces) is discovering that we have access to and may use, the very creative power that made our world.

Whether or not you are Christian, we suggest finding a bible and reading the first chapter, Genesis 1. "And God said, Let there be . . . and it was so." Whether you regard it as factual or metaphor, the principle holds. That principle is *creation by the word.* Any word is an idea in form. Any idea in form, given sufficient uncontaminated attention/energy/intention, will manifest. This is the essence of personal power for which Pluto is the symbol.

The key to efficient use of Pluto is not willpower, but willingness-power. It is the willingness to consciously channel Divine creative power through your life. It is the willingness to recognize that we are no longer the *little children of God*, but the adult children of Deity. It is time to *be about Our Father's business.*

Pluto's message is simple:

We are the creators of the future.

We will create it, as we believe in our power to do so.

We will create magically, from an idea, a word.

As Original Being created a place for its offspring,

So we continue creating for ours.

Pluto in the Elements and Signs

Pluto in Fire

Pluto in fire is spiritual power, which is really that power which attaches to our sense of identity. We can do _____ because we are_____. For many generations humans have believed themselves to be limited by their physical forms. Overtly or covertly, this was linked to the notion of humans as *higher animals*. Although we sometimes used the phrase *children of God*, we did not really believe that we were born of Spirit. We thought of ourselves more as *created beings*, than *divinely procreated beings*.

During the Piscean Age, what was called Christ Consciousness arose. Its main expression took the form of thinking of ourselves as little children of Deity. With the Aquarian Age comes *God Consciousness*. It means realizing that, as offspring of a God/dess, we can only be gods and goddesses. It means realizing that humanity is growing up, as it was designed to do. It means that the time has come for humanity to begin sharing the task of ongoing creation. It means reclaiming our right to *speak our word*, and *make it so.*

Aries: Aries is Son of Man. By the time of the next Pluto transit of Aries, humanity will come into is full spiritual heritage. Remember, this is the title most often used by Jesus ben Joseph, some 2000 years ago.

Aries Pluto is catalytic power, the power to quicken. It symbolizes the powerful urge that produces inception, the initial push of pioneering ideas and actions. The writer believes that this will be the first generation of the next age, the driving force that powers the final transformation of humanity into a new form, capable of feats never before seen.

Leo: Leo is Son/Daughter of God/dess. Leo Pluto is identified with the creative aspect of Divinity, and realizes certain talents implied by it. Leo is about actions and roles and literally translates to Deity playing human roles.

During the last Leo transit, Pluto restricted the idea of spiritual genetics in a small portion of the population. Remember that Leo is a fixed sign, so Plutonian power sometimes almost blasted individuals out of roles inherited from their *merely human family*.

Sagittarius: Sagittarius is about beliefs, and the publication/broadcasting of them. Today, huge media campaigns are designed to influence our beliefs about health and politics. Drug companies do their utmost to spread disease-beliefs because it sells drugs. Publicity surrounding elections makes it impossible for government to function constitutionally, while so-called *patriotism* is used to dismantle what is left of democracy. This is the result of centuries in which individuals gave up their power to choose to others who claimed to be wiser.

Sagittarius Pluto confronts us with the results of ill-chosen beliefs. We are seeing the consequences of accepting opinion as truth. Those consequences have resulted in wars and rumors of wars, as old men send young ones out to die in the name of their gods. Advertising campaigns have also resulted in incredibly high rates of cardio-vascular problems and cancer. It is high time to look at what we are creating in our lives.

When transiting Pluto crossed the Galactic Center, it aligned the personal power potential of humanity with a kind of worm-hole or direct channel to the higher truths held in the mind of Deity. Scattered across the landscape of Earth, individuals began tapping into knowledge beyond the parameters of dreams held by earlier generations.

Much of the current turmoil is the result of Sagittarian exaggeration, and we are called to notice the difference between past history and future potential. If it is true that humanity created the problems, it is equally true that we can create the solutions. Pluto's transit of the Galactic Center awakened the messengers and teachers to show us how.

Pluto in Earth

Pluto in earth is contained power, energy stored in form. It points to the fact that energy and mass are equal and interchangeable. Form is simply concentrated and compounded energy, compressed inside a boundary created by consciousness. Hence, form becomes a storage place for power. In some sense, every physical construct may be seen as a battery.

Taurus: Taurus Pluto is fixed and might be called the power of tenacity or stubbornness. It reminds us that fixed intention is a creative force. The ultimate power of Taurus Pluto is the power of evaluation. No matter how tenacious you are in your creative efforts, if the object of your prayer is not properly evaluated, nothing can happen.

Virgo: Virgo Pluto is mutable, rather like alternating current. It also involves choice, selection, and efficiency. Its most efficient use is to carefully select your goals based on personal usefulness. If you are to create efficiently, you must focus only on acquiring that for which you have a use. Plutonian power cannot be used to create anything useless or dysfunctional.

A secondary aspect of this refers to the power inherent in practice. Abilities are acquired and improved with practice.

Capricorn: Capricorn Pluto refers to the limits of power as set by human maturation. Only as we mature do we expand our beliefs about what we have the power to do/have/be/become. Capricorn Pluto is limited by our belief in what is possible to humanity, to what is possible to us while in body.

Historically, people have tried to *get out of body*, assuming that it would expand their creative powers. They did not realize that what is possible in one form is equally possible in every form.

Any placement in Capricorn is intended to redefine the word *human*, to include our divine genetic gifts. Today's Pluto transit of Capricorn is increasing incidents in which humans do the improbable, even the *impossible*. Once the improbable reaches a certain level, the *impossible becomes possible*, and eventually routine.

Pluto in Air

Pluto in air is intellectual power, as an aspect of human consciousness. It is the *breath of life*, breathed into animate man to produce a living soul. Ultimately, it is conscious power, literally the power of the word, thought, idea, belief.

Gemini: Gemini Pluto is magical, referring to the power of knowing the name of a thing. It also reminds us that we must name that thing good, for we can never create what we call evil. Evil can only be a pseudonym, imposed after the fact. All initial creation is good.

Libra: Libra Pluto refers to the balance of power and the power available through the partnership between Deity and humanity. It also points to judgement, and the fact that as we judge others, so we judge ourselves. We may share power, for mutual ends, but we must never attempt to use it against others, because the pendulum-of-power will surely swing back, and knock us down.

Aquarius: Aquarius Pluto is the power of group consciousness. Where ideas are held in weak energy, as hopes or wishes, when concentrated over a long period of time, or in the minds of multiple individuals, creation will be made manifest. Aquarius Pluto is the *hope of tomorrow*, the unlimited potential for developing ever greater personal power.

Pluto in Water

Pluto in water is emotional power. Like any fluid, it takes on the shape of the container. Emotions are the spontaneous actions which accompany feelings. Feelings are the mind of the body; they tell us what we need. Pluto transforms our idea of *body* to include our heritage as offspring of Father God and Mother Earth. Pluto in water refers to the personal power/ability to have, attract or create all of our needs–both physical and spiritual.

Cancer: Pluto in Cancer is a reborn need system. In this generation, the awareness of spiritual needs was reborn. This was a new human impulse, heralded by the discovery of Pluto in 1930. Under it, a few began to expand their sense of *family* and the concept of a *family of choice* was born. More importantly, the idea of being offspring of Deity was reborn in a small portion of this generation. They became the seeds that led to the current rise in consciousness.

Scorpio: Pluto in Scorpio is at its most intense. Transformation or Investment must occur. Each native is destined for an *investment of power* which transforms the life. It may be as simple as freeing oneself from a family or relationship that has been draining our energy. It may also lead natives to a true *calling*, for each has the potential to be a priest/tess and/or magician.

The great revelation of this phase was the backlash of power created by negative judgments on human sexuality. Never before had so many died in the name of sexual judgment.

Pisces: Pluto in Pisces is mastered power, often referred as miracle power. In this placement is contained all the creative, transformative, and healing potential invested in every person born. As we master Life, as we learn full mastery of consciousness, an ocean of power becomes available and our potential rises to limitless heights. When Pluto next transits Pisces, the co-creative powers of humanity will extend beyond our current horizons of thought or perception. Then, out of that power, a new birth of humanity will arise, and all the world will begin a cycle of development that lies beyond our current ability to imagine.